JOURNEY OF HOPE

Love, Marriage, and Overcoming Infertility at 40

To Diana,

Thank you for being
a part of my journey!
Wish you many blessings!!

Samantha Fitts

11-8-18

by
Samantha Fitts, Ed.D.

First published by Dog Ear Publishing
4011 Vincennes Road
Indianapolis, IN 46268
www.dogearpublishing.net

ISBN: 978-145756-495-6

This book is printed on acid-free paper.
Printed in the United States of America

Table of Contents

Dedication

This book is dedicated to the loving memory of my father, Mack Arthur Rogers. I know he would be proud of me. It is also dedicated to:

> my daughter, Nadia Grace, who is my hope and gift from God;
> my husband, Elroy Jevon, who is committed to our vows and always there for me in sickness and in health;
> my mother, Nellie;
> my sisters, Serena and Danielle;
> my father in law, Eddie O.;
> my brother and sister in law, Eddie G. and Mary;
> my nephews, Mackell, Simeon, and Jared;
> my nieces, Brooklyn and Amelia.

I thank them all for their love and support.

Acknowledgements

I thank God for giving me the wisdom to complete this book so that I might inspire others. Special thanks are extended to Diana Porter, David Shands, and Marcus Y. Rosier for encouraging me to write this book. I thank my family, friends, sorority sisters, and co-workers for their prayers and support over the years. In addition, my gratitude goes to my minister, Dr. Kelvin Teamer, and my church family at the Bouldercrest Church of Christ for their ongoing encouragement. Finally, I am appreciative for the support given to me by the staff at Dendera Cosmetic Studio in the West End of Atlanta, my doula Teresa Howard, founder of Labor of Love Doula & Childbirth Services, the midwives at Intown Midwifery, and the many compassionate nurses and doctors at Atlanta Medical Center.

Introduction

Are you living the life you envisioned? Take a moment, close your eyes, and take a deep breath. Now think back to the time when you were young and asked the following questions: What do I want to be when I grow up? Do I want to get married and have children? What are my overall goals in life?

What were your answers to these questions? I'm going to share mine with you so you can take a journey with me throughout the pages of this book, one that is about living the life that you want, the one that contains the answer to those questions you just thought about. I've come to realize that nothing is impossible if one is determined and confident. In my case, I've also realized that all things are possible with God, and my own journey could not have been undertaken without his help. There were so many coincidences that I believe in my heart that God was using my determination to work wonders in my life. As you'll see, some things that happened to me are hard to explain without the concept of divine intervention. If you have a different belief system, that's okay. Read my story and apply what works for *you*. Either way, I'm confident you can benefit from my experiences. And who knows? You might find yourself adopting an entirely new way to look at life. As I said, I believe anything can happen.

Personally, I wanted an education, a good job, a comfortable life, and to get married and have children. It didn't happen all at once, however. It took time, and there were difficulties along the way, difficulties that would cause discouragement in just about anyone. I guess you can say I wanted the fairy tale, the one in which everything falls into place at exactly the right time with exactly the right people.

But fairy tales can sometimes be frightening, and some even have a few gremlins and monsters along the way.

Are you ready to hear about my *own* tale?

When I was in my mid-thirties I began to reflect on the answers to my questions. I began to check off what I had accomplished: Go to college? Check. Become a teacher? Check. Live in a big city? Check. Drive a nice car? Check. Live in a two-story house? Check. Get married? Well, more on that later. Have children? There was definitely no check for this question, and by the time I reached my late thirties I was disappointed about the lack of success in accomplishing my childhood goal of having children. Like most young girls, I dreamed of having a family, especially since I had several aunts and uncles, all of whom had children. I was surrounded by family and children from the time I was a youngster. And yet there I was, thirty-four years old and living in Atlanta, but I wasn't married and had no children even though, in these modern times, not being married doesn't deter some women from getting pregnant. My biological clock was ticking loudly, but I preferred to be married when I conceived.

I was living the life I envisioned in part, but not totally. Don't get me wrong. It took perseverance to go to college and get a good job in the field I'd chosen. Not all college graduates are so blessed as I was, and not all drove nice cars or owned their own homes. I was grateful for what I had. A lot of dreams from my early musings had come true, but something was missing. A majority of females grow up to get married and have children. In a sense, it's the culmination of all other life events and the glue that cements the other elements together. Some people are content to go through life without a partner, but I wasn't one of them. Friends, co-workers, and family members continually asked me when I was going to settle down, marry, and have kids, and by the time I was well into adulthood, listening to these inquiries were growing wearisome. I didn't want to hear them anymore. These people meant well, but I'd been dating and no serious relationship had grown to fruition. The fairy tale wasn't complete.

A large part of my story is about putting that last piece into the puzzle, about finding the last element that would enable me to say that I was truly living the life I had envisioned: having a child. But one doesn't just walk into a store and pick out a husband and baby and charge it all on a credit card. There are online dating sites, but contrary to what some television commercials say, they're no guarantee for success.

The hardest part of my journey, and what most of the following pages are devoted to, was finding the right husband and having children. But why is having children hard, you might ask. The answer is that there are many fertility issues for women in their mid-to-late thirties, and getting pregnant isn't a given. Throughout this book, you'll find summaries and points to remember as you read about my personal odyssey. They pertain to setting and achieving goals, but most of all they are designed to help you fulfill your own dreams and live the life you envision. That includes getting married and having a baby. More specifically, my story is about having a baby later in life, a time when it becomes statistically harder to become pregnant. If your biological clock is ticking, this book is for you!

But I'm getting ahead of myself. Let me tell you a little more about who I am since everyone's life is a tapestry, and each thread is important in creating the big picture. Let's start at the beginning.

CHAPTER ONE

Waiting to Have Children

I was born in the seventies in the town of Opp, Alabama, and grew up in another small town, Enterprise, Alabama. I had a large family and was constantly surrounded by aunts, uncles, and cousins. My mother had two brothers and five sisters. My father had seven brothers and four sisters. Most of my aunts and uncles had children (one of my aunts had fifteen children), so I had a virtual army of cousins. We were close since most of them lived in Enterprise, although I saw cousins who lived in Opp and other states at least once a year. Therefore, from the very beginning of my life family was very important. For me, that's what life was all about. I guess you could say that nineteen aunts and uncles and dozens of cousins gave new meaning to the term extended family.

Faith in God was also instilled in me from an early age— we were a church-going family—and the members of my church were an extension of my biological family. We were there for each other the way I believe God is always there for me—and always has been. I was baptized when I was nine years old at the Adams Street Church of Christ in Enterprise. Baptism is a sign that we enter into a relationship with God, and while many people fall away as they grow older, for me it was the beginning of a lifelong experience.

That's not to say that I thought life was trouble-free. Surrounded by such a large family, I witnessed many good relationships as well as some that were not so successful. It was all part of that tapestry I mentioned. There's good and bad in the world, and we have to deal with all of it. My father died when I was twelve and my mother remarried, although she later divorced. These kinds of events are a part of life, but as I look back, the good always outweighed the bad. In fact, there were some things about which I became absolutely passionate about.

I was still very young when I developed a love of sports. We lived in a two-bedroom home, and my father was an avid Atlanta Braves fan. At the time, TBS, the television network was run by Braves' owner Ted Turner, and their games were broadcast nationally every night at eight o'clock. I didn't really want to go to bed at eight—what child does?—so it was either watch baseball on the one television set we had or go to sleep. I chose the Atlanta Braves, and my father, uncles, and cousins all taught me about the game. As time went on, I knew the rules of the game as well the players, stats, and so much more. I was a fan!

I also developed a love of football, and my favorite franchise growing up was the Dallas Cowboys, known as "America's team." Football was also an integral part of the culture of Enterprise, as it is in so many towns across America when the glow of stadium lights can be seen shortly after sunset. High school football was big, and it was a case of Friday Night Lights during the fall in Enterprise. Like most people, I attended the games and was invested in the home team. Just like family and faith, baseball and Friday Night Lights were part of the rhythms of life. But it didn't end there. I also participated in sports and played basketball in junior high school and softball at the local recreation center. I still love sports today, and it all started with a single television set and some high school football games.

I had other passions as well, and one remains with me to this day—my love of radio, television, film, and theatre. My acting interests developed at church when performing in skits for various programs. I was also a member of the drama club in high school. The drama club was sponsored by Ms. Wingate, my eleventh grade teacher who was an actress. Sure, we had sports in Enterprise, but it was still a small town, not a big city sprawling with shopping malls, cultural attractions, and multiplex theaters. So I was also planted in front of our television set to watch *The Cosby Show*, *A Different World*, and more sitcoms and shows than I can name here. They were comedies, of course, but they also showed strong family connections. As in my own life, the relationships depicted on these shows weren't free of conflict, so I could identify with the episodes I watched. There were good times in the Huxtable family, but they coped and made it through many difficulties, too.

My love of the broadcast medium didn't stop with sitcoms, however. I was a huge fan of Arsenio Hall and Oprah Winfrey. Arsenio would come out and wave his fist in circles over his head as his live studio audience went wild. He was funny and had a variety of great guests from all walks of life and the entertainment world. He also had musical guests on every program, and I had already become a big consumer of music videos when stations like MTV, VH1, and BET were essentially music video stations, playing videos by various artists twenty-four seven. When it came to recording artists, Michael Jackson was number one in my book. His music and dancing were phenomenal, and some say that he may have been the most talented musician of all time. I suppose that opinion is subjective but I recall feeling disbelief when I heard he'd died years later in 2009.

And then there was Oprah, one of the most prestigious and well-known celebrities in the world—and her fame and reputation have only increased. She interviewed celebrities, too, but she also had theme programs with panelists, many of them ordinary people, discussing important everyday issues, from relationships to spirituality to health to books. Oprah's show was about life, and there was no subject she wasn't willing to tackle as she walked among her audience and solicited questions for her onstage guests. I eventually met her, and got to attend one of her shows, but that comes later on in this book.

In general, I was a careful observer of what I watched. I examined the credits of television shows as they rolled at the end of programs, and I was interested in the job titles that scrolled on the screen in front of me. I wondered what these people did—producers, directors, lighting technicians, sound mixers, gaffers, and stage managers. I wrote letters to the people on these shows, much of it fan mail, and occasionally received a response. If I did get an answer, such as a letter or an autographed picture, I knew they weren't personalized and sent only to me, but a few were, and that was exciting. As I got older, I thought it would be interesting to have a job in the broadcasting industry, whether it was radio or TV.

I, therefore, had many interests while growing up, and being enthusiastic about so many things made me to want to expand my life beyond small-town living. I knew there was a bigger world out there, and I wanted to be part of it. For as far back as I can remember, I've always been goal oriented, and my goal was to attend college, major in education, teach, and eventually get married and have a family of my own. I wasn't counting on having fifteen children, mind you, but it was an important part of the life I saw in my mind's eye. The other occupations that I observed in Enterprise were doctor and lawyer, occupations that can flourish almost anywhere, but as you can see from my early childhood experiences, I'd always been interested in learning. I thought that being a teacher was a rewarding profession—I had great teachers who I looked up to because they inspired me—and knew that I would both love teaching and be good at it. I'd become a "lifelong learner"—the ultimate goal for any student—and I wanted to inspire others to be the same. I still loved radio and television—the lure of working in these industries never completely vanished—but I knew how hard it would be to break into these jobs let alone bring in a steady paycheck with which I could support myself. Even famous actors have been starving artists who waited tables and lived in studio apartments for many years before getting their big break.

From 1994 to 1997, I attended college at Alabama State University, a Historically Black College and University (HBCU) in Montgomery, AL. I pledged Alpha Kappa Alpha Sorority, Incorporated (AKA). Mrs. Jones, my fourth grade teacher and one of my favorite teachers was an AKA and because of her, I wanted to be a member of such an illustrious organization. Alpha Kappa Alpha Sorority, Inc. will always hold a special place in my heart. I developed lifelong bonds with a special group of women who share the same interest for the sorority and support for one another. I also met many great people, some of whom I remain in touch with today. I attended church at times, worked a lot, and focused on earning my degree and moving to Atlanta—the big city! I graduated Magna Cum Laude with a Bachelor's Degree in Special Education. During my senior year, I met recruiters from the Atlanta area at college job fairs, and my prospects looked good. It had been a long journey from my two-bedroom home in Enterprise, watching Oprah and Arsenio, and dreaming about all the endless possibilities in the world, but I'd succeeded in fulfilling many of my goals and putting those checkmarks next to the aspirations I'd had when envisioning the kind of life I wanted. But I wasn't all the way there, at least not yet. There was still time and I wasn't worried. I knew what I could do when I set my mind to it, so there was no hurry to complete the portrait I saw in my imagination. I had a lot of time left to check off the rest of the boxes.

Also, God had my back. I was sure of it.

In January 1998, I moved to Atlanta after completing my student teaching and became a big Falcons fan in the process! I didn't waste any time in taking the next steps in building my career and started teaching in the Atlanta metro area while attending graduate school at Georgia State University. In order to continue to nourish my faith and rededicate myself to God, I placed my membership at Bouldercrest Church of Christ in Atlanta and became involved in the youth and singles ministries there. I'd always read the Bible and I taught Sunday school to students starting with pre-K. I helped organize events for the youth ministry as well as compiled study guides for the Bible Bowl teams that competed in quizzes on scripture much like scholastic quiz bowl teams compete academically in many cities. I'd been part of a Bible Bowl team myself when I was younger, and I enjoyed coaching our youth and chaperoning trips when the team went on the road. As for the singles ministry, it wasn't designed with the intent of single people meeting each other in order to date as much as it was for bible study, camaraderie and companionship, such as watching sporting events together. Years later, I still encounter some of the kids from the youth ministry who are now in their twenties. It's always rewarding to see my students from the past and they serve to remind me that I'm on the right path in my career and that I made a difference in the lives of others.

However, I still wasn't finished with my education. In 2000, I received a Master's degree in Special Education at age twenty-five. I then earned an Education Specialist degree in Leadership through a weekend program at Lincoln Memorial University in Tennessee. From 2005 to 2009, I obtained my doctorate in Educational Leadership from the Atlanta campus of Argosy University.

I'd made a conscious decision to pursue teaching and had received my terminal degree after many hard years of work, but that didn't mean that my passion for radio and television work had diminished. That goal was always in the background, always claiming my attention in some way, shape, or form, and at this time in my life, I pursued it as a hobby. I worked as an extra in films being shot in the Atlanta area. I was in *The Gospel* and *Motives*, and was also a featured extra in an episode of *Meet the Browns* titled "Meet the Trainer." Additionally, I was part of the opening for the 2006 *Black Movie Awards* hosted by Tyler Perry and directed by the accomplished Suzanne de Passe.

I also worked with a radio personality. I scheduled this well-known figure by taking requests for him to make personal appearances in the area since he was quite famous and always in demand. I also arranged for school classes, athletic teams, and coaches to visit the station and, at times, was allowed to be on the air. Handling his calendar and booking appearances was enjoyable since I was part of something that had grabbed my attention in a big way when I was growing up. Since my primary job was teaching, I guess you could say that I was having my cake and eating it, too.

I also did a voiceover and my pictures were used for a topic featured on *Oprah* in 2000. I looked at her website and responded to the question "Are you ready for the holidays? Are you dreading going home?" Many people encounter tension when their extended families gather for Christmas and, coming from a big family, I thought I'd see if the producers wanted to use my reflections on the topic. My personal family experiences had been predominantly positive, but I believed I could contribute to the segment by relating my own perspective. I could have said to myself that it was a real long shot that they would use me, but that's not who I am. It was one more way in which my passion for the industry found an outlet.

Teaching, attending graduate school, and pursuing my hobby were exhilarating, and some people might say that I was "living the dream." In a sense I was, but I was now thirty-four. People began to ask me more and more when I was going to marry, settle down, and start a family. I'd been dating since my college years, and although I'd made a conscious decision not to get married before the age of thirty, I was open to breaking that rule if a college sweetheart came along and swept me off my feet. For better or worse, it didn't happen.

I'd dated through regular channels but also used online dating. I even tried long distance dating after meeting people online, and a few men came to Atlanta to meet me, but nothing serious ever developed. In fact, Mr. Right didn't come along as a result of *any* kind of dating, online or otherwise. The questions from my family and friends escalated in frequency as to when I was going to put the final brush strokes on the picture that was my life up until that point, but I had no answer and at times grew even wearier of the inquiries. The real answer was that nothing was working out . . . yet. That didn't mean that I'd given up. It was more of a case that it just wasn't meant to be during all of the years I'd dedicated to establishing my career.

That having been said, I knew that time was moving on and that my biological clock was ticking. It wasn't too late to start a family, and statistics show that women and young adults in general wait longer these days to marry and settle down, but I had a strong desire to achieve these goals. It was time.

Summary and Points to Remember
I was born in a small town without the opportunities available in larger communities but I had a clear vision of what I wanted. Because I set goals and held fast to their realization, I achieved success in my career. Not only did I begin teaching and acquire advanced degrees in education, but I also participated in local church activities, dated, and made time for my hobby in radio broadcasting

and acting. I didn't have everything I wanted yet, but I didn't adopt a mindset of defeat.

Here's what I want you to learn and implement in your own life.

- Set clear goals and be a goal-oriented person.
- Visualize what you want and take the concrete steps to make your goals happen, both for your career and in your personal life.
- Nurture hobbies and dreams, such as I did with radio, television, film, and theatre. You never can tell where they might lead you. They're enjoyable and part of who you are.
- Don't be afraid to "put yourself out there," whether it's through dating, writing fan mail, or working with youth or other segments of the population. You'll meet interesting people and experience a sense of accomplishment.
- Be open to furthering your career through advanced degrees, ongoing education courses, seminars, or seeking promotions. The old adage is true: Nothing ventured, nothing gained.
- Don't expect everything to happen at once. Life is a journey. If you find that time has passed and you still don't have the complete life you've envisioned, don't give up. You're never too old to take that next step, change careers, or learn how to achieve your goals.
- If your belief system allows it, find strength in God and faith. Become active in a church so that you can share your experiences and dreams with a wider community and also draw sustenance and courage from them in return. Everything is possible with God, and staying connected to him gives you greater strength for anything you choose to do.

CHAPTER TWO

The Next Step

Having successfully defended my dissertation to become Dr. Samantha Rogers, my prayer to God was "I'm ready to get married and start a family." Jesus said, "Ask and you shall receive," and I believed the verse meant what it said. To me, faith and the Bible weren't just matters that people dealt with on Sunday, but rather represented the ways a person should live his or her life. I made this simple, straightforward prayer, expecting that it would come to pass. I didn't know *how* it would since I was learning the hard way that a good man is hard to find. I'd met lots of nice men while dating, but that special someone hadn't materialized yet. By May of 2009, I stopped dating altogether since nothing seemed to be happening on that front. I didn't want to pay out more money on internet dating sites, hoping instead that I might meet someone the old-fashioned way, like at the produce section of the grocery store. A lot of men are known to open conversation with comments like "Gee, I don't know if this melon is ripe" or "Are these tomatoes too soft?" And if I didn't meet anyone at the grocery store, I could encounter a lot of people in day-to-day life. Maybe I'd meet an educator or some other professional. After all, the internet has only been around for a little while and yet people have been marrying and having children for thousands of years. Why not me? It was worth a try.

My taxman at the time was in his nineties, and even though I only saw him during tax season, he was a powerful and wise man who advised me as much on life as he did on tax matters. He'd been married for fifty years and told me that even though I hadn't found a husband yet after years of dating, I should have faith and that I would eventually find the right person. It's wonderful when life puts such people in our path, and I was inclined to follow his advice.

I'd seen Steve Harvey on *Oprah*—yes, I was still watching—and saw him promoting a book called *Act Like a Lady, Think Like a Man: What Men Really Think About Love, Relationships, Intimacy, and Commitment*. I bought the book since it had a lot of advice for women who were looking for the right man and not necessarily having a lot of luck. The book's viewpoint was both honest and humorous, with Harvey's trademark wit mixed in with his advice. His approach was that women had to get inside the minds of men and understand how they thought and acted, which wasn't always apparent to a woman in search of Mr. Right. The book talked about sex, children, dating, and various male personality types. Overall, Harvey maintained that women were clueless as to what motivated men and that they got away with whatever they could. In essence, he took the self-deprecating approach that men act like dogs. It was interesting to me that Harvey also wrote about women who were independent-minded, which certainly described me. I devoured the book since it had such practical advice on meeting and marrying your perfect mate.

I got back into dating in a rather unusual way. I'd bought a townhouse in 2003—my first home as a result of enjoying professional success. Four years later, that house became rental property since I purchased a five-bedroom house with a two-car garage. Atlanta has a lot of successful women, and it's not uncommon for them to buy their own homes. The thinking is basically "I can't sit around and wait for a man to show up!" That was my thinking as well.

By August of 2009, my tenant decided not to renew his lease, and I was searching for a new one for the rental property. I looked at a popular online site that lists just about anything one can search for, and while I was looking for prospective tenants, the dating section caught my eye. Since I'd previously engaged in online dating, I thought I'd read a few of the profiles for the Atlanta metro area just out of curiosity. Many looked like the "same ole, same ole." Some of the men posted very graphic pictures, as if they were probably looking for "one thing". Others just didn't resonate with me. One, however, caught my eye. The profile had a picture of the man's face (not all of them did), and he appeared to be a handsome gentleman not afraid of showing who he was. In general, the profile spoke of a decent man looking for a decent woman. He stated he had a job, no children, never been married, had his own townhouse and own transportation. He even said that curves were okay. I emailed him and attached my picture. I wasn't paying money to an online dating service, so I thought it was worth a try. I had nothing to lose. You can't catch a fish unless you throw your line in the water.

We met in August of 2009 after we'd emailed each other for a few weeks. He was a nice man and we met at a mutually agreed upon location since it was our first date and saw the movie *G. I. Joe*. The date went okay, but I didn't hear back from him and deleted his number from my cell phone, thinking he wasn't interested. Out of the blue, he texted me in November when the Falcons played the Cowboys, but again there was no follow-up. He called and left a message on December 27, 2009 which I returned on January 1, 2010. We made plans to attend a college football championship game in January, but we had to cancel because of extreme flooding in the area.

As it turned out, Elroy was indeed interested in going out with me. We watched NFL playoff games at Dave and Buster's Arcade—public areas are the best places to meet when you're getting to know someone you've met online—and then went to see the movie *Avatar*. After that, we started seeing each other on weekends to go to the movies or watch football games, and I eventually invited him to my house. He would make the one-hour drive across town for our dates and he always drove home, putting no pressure on me to stay the night. If we went anywhere else, he always picked me up and was a perfect gentleman, even to the point of opening the door for me. Chivalry wasn't dead.

It was still early in our relationship, and I wasn't sure how Elroy felt about me even though I couldn't fault him for anything. I was still consulting Steve Harvey's book from time to time on how to evaluate men, and I told a good friend that "Steve Harvey said this and Steve Harvey said that" and that I wasn't positive if this was the right relationship. Her response was, "Girl, put that book down! You're getting discouraged for no reason." In other words, dating wasn't necessarily a matter of checking off advice from a how-to book, so I decided to let our courtship evolve naturally. Things seemed to be going well, so I took a break away from the book.

By the summer of 2010, we officially became a couple, vacationing together at a resort in Florida. We were comfortable in each other's presence, and I could see that Elroy was honest, considerate, and intelligent (he was a telecom engineer), and we decided to see each other exclusively. He also wasn't carrying any personal baggage, which is a rarity among many people, and that was a big plus. He told his family about me and when I talked to his brother on the phone, he said that Elroy rarely took off work to go on vacation. He'd been telling me the truth. He really *did* work a lot!

In August 2010, I traveled to Littleton, North Carolina, to meet Elroy's family. Littleton is a small rural town, and Elroy's extended family lived out in the country on land where they'd grown up for generations. Things went well, although his family swarmed around me, especially his aunt, to ask if we'd set a wedding date yet. "When is the wedding?" she asked several times, adding that she wasn't going to be around much longer. They were understandably eager for us to tie the knot, but they were getting a little bit ahead of the normal progression of our relationship. We'd only made the decision to become a couple two months earlier.

My mother was also very happy that we were dating and felt that a ring from Elroy would be forthcoming. In September, however, she was diagnosed with breast cancer and had to undergo chemotherapy and radiation. I was understandably distressed at a time when I was becoming hopeful that Elroy and I *would* one day get married. I tried to remain positive that my mother would recover since I wanted her to be able to share in my future should Elroy decide to propose. I was cautiously optimistic about this possibility, but I put my mother's illness and my future with Elroy into the hands of God. Happily, my mother was in remission by August of 2011.

We continued dating and since the relationship was serious, I expected that Elroy would sooner or later give me a ring and ask me to marry him. I knew he was the right person, so in my mind it was a question of "when," not "if." Maybe, I thought, it would be on some special day since it was now fall and the holidays were approaching.

We spent Christmas with Elroy's family in Littleton, and his brother said, "Wow, he must be really serious about you since the two of you are staying here together. It's a bold move!" I was hopeful and thought that maybe this was going to be the time when Elroy would decide to make our relationship permanent, a life spent together. I would finally be able to check off the last two elements of the life I'd envisioned since I was young. If I didn't get the ring at Christmas, then it would probably be on Valentine's Day. To me, it was a fait accompli, a matter of time.

Elroy's family had an endearing habit of going to bed early on Christmas Eve so they could wake up early Christmas morning, exchange gifts, and eat breakfast. There I was, watching everyone exchange gifts on this festive morning, and Elroy handed me a gift bag from Macy's and a gift bag from Bath and Body Works. Well, I thought, I guess it really *will* be Valentine's Day or New Year's

Eve before I get a proposal. I reached into the gift bags and found perfumes and assorted bath oils. I thanked him, but he asked me if I were sure there was nothing else in the bag. I looked, but I saw only tissue.

"Well, maybe you should look again," he advised.

I dug down into the tissue and found an engagement ring beneath the tissue on which the perfume and bath oils had been placed. Elroy then got down on one knee and asked me if I would marry him. I didn't hesitate for a second.

"Yes!" I exclaimed.

Elroy's family was totally surprised. He hadn't even told his father, who he was afraid might have spilled the beans. His sister-in-law, who chided Elroy that she could have helped in the planning, asked if she could quickly get her camera. The only person besides myself who'd been suspicious had been his brother, and he'd been right. Bringing me home and letting me stay with him under the same roof had been a signal that it was going to happen. To celebrate our engagement, his dad took out the fine china dinnerware set to serve the traditional Christmas breakfast.

When Valentine's Day finally rolled around, it was all the more special since we were engaged. Elroy sent me flowers and Shari's berries, which are strawberries dipped in gourmet chocolate and other treats. I was very happy, as was my mother, who felt better during her cancer treatments since she was overjoyed that the rest of my dreams were coming true.

The months ahead were busy, but Elroy and I still had good times and lived our lives. We loved to travel and went to Los Angeles in March and to New Orleans in May to attend the wedding of a friend of Elroy's (who would officially be the last of his "crew" to get married). The J Crew, as they called themselves, consisted of Jason, Jacques, and Jevon, the latter being Elroy's middle name, which is what some people call him. They'd grown up and attended college together and it had been Jason who'd suggested that Elroy post a dating profile on the popular internet site where I'd found him.

I also had a chance to check off another item on my bucket list, which was to attend the taping of *Oprah* for the first time. In April, Patricia McRae, my sorority sister, and I went to the "The Last Ever Harpo Hookup" show. These shows were for avid Oprah fans and I'd sent letters and emails to the producers over the years. I was rewarded with tickets for one of the final hookup tapings. These Oprah shows were exciting for several reasons. Harpo Hookups selected fans who had dreams that ordinarily would be beyond anyone's reach, but Oprah has a way of making things happen. On the hookup shows, fans could meet their favorite celebrities, attend basketball games with Shaquille O'Neal, play golf with Justin Timberlake, dance with the Rockettes, and do just about anything. Moreover, every member of the studio audience received a gift somehow related to what the fan herself was receiving. When I was at the show in Chicago, the fan was awarded a dream wedding at Disney. In turn, everybody in the audience received a bag with some kind of Disney-related merchandise. These hookup shows are best remembered for the time Oprah gave everyone in the audience an automobile. I wasn't that lucky, but I had fulfilled a dream of my own by just being at the show.

Elroy turned thirty-six in April and I turned thirty-six in May. I had always said that I would have my first baby by the age of forty, so I was still on the right track. There had been a couple of bumps in the road, but thanks to meeting Elroy—he had turned out to be the perfect mate—I was still on schedule. Elroy had been in the right place at the right time, and I knew that God had things well in hand.

During the months following our engagement, there was a lot of wedding planning that needed to be done. As it turned out, Elroy and I didn't have any idea as to what a wedding cost and thought we should shop around for the best price. We'd gone to see Pristine Chapel Lakeside the week after I'd received my ring on Christmas Day since we were off work for the holidays. Back in 2008, I'd attended the wedding of a co-worker at this site and as soon as I entered the foyer, I had two thoughts. The first was that the chapel was beautiful. My second was that this was where I, too, would one day get married. The chapel was elegant, but the grounds on which the facility was located were beautiful as well, and there was even a lake with a fountain. The biggest advantage of having a wedding there was that they offered a price that included everything anyone needed, meaning that it was a package deal. They provided the food, cake, flowers, photography, chapel, and a professional staff to take the worry out of the event so that a couple could enjoy their wedding day. The amenities included crystal, china, flatware, centerpieces, and linen tablecloths in an elegant and peaceful rural setting. We'd stopped shopping around since paying for all of the above amenities on an a la carte basis would have amounted to more than the cost offered by the Pristine Chapel. The chapel clearly offered the best value for the full range of services that one expects at a wedding.

The choice of a wedding venue, however, was only one consideration. We had to line up groomsmen, bridesmaids, and flower girls, and these details were arranged between January and September of 2011. But there was more. Jennie, my real estate agent and matron of honor, suggested that we have an engagement barbecue for family, friends and the wedding party, and I expected a small cookout—nothing elaborate. Instead, she threw an enormous barbecue with a lot of friends, family, a live singer and food. Finally, On August 21, my cousin Pamela, my sister Danielle, and my mother Nellie hosted my bridal shower that was held a little over a month away from my scheduled wedding date. We had a great time playing games to see how well everyone knew the bride to be.

The big day was on September 24, 2011. I'd booked an entire block of rooms at a nearby hotel since the wedding was scheduled to start at twelve thirty in the afternoon, and Atlanta traffic can get gridlocked very quickly due to roadwork or other problems. With another wedding scheduled later in the day, the staff told me that the service would begin on time. At the hotel, I'd be just five minutes away from the chapel. The wedding party, mother, and family all stayed there and that morning, Eric, my hair stylist, and Deevetkeio, my makeup artist, came to the hotel to style everyone. I took my personal pictures before the ceremony. We ran a little behind schedule and the pictures with the bridesmaids were postponed until after the ceremony. I was getting tense by this point, and with all the rushing I'd turned into a little bit of a bridezilla.

By twelve thirty, however, everything was in place and I was walking down the aisle—I became nervous. I'd had control of the entire process for the past several months, but now that it was time to go through with the wedding, I was no longer in control. It wasn't a question of cold feet since I loved Elroy very much, but suddenly all eyes were on me and I had to let the ceremony proceed. I trembled at the altar, Elroy had to squeeze my hand to let me know everything was going to be all right. I'd had a classic case of stage fright.

With the minister, Deandrea (my cousin), presiding, Elroy and I exchanged vows at the Pristine Chapel during a lovely ceremony. It was every bit as special as I'd dreamed—and more. Chandra Currelley and Vincent Tolbert sang at the ceremony, and William Green was the pianist. The jazz band PR Experience performed at the reception which was great, thanks to the staff of Pristine Chapel who delivered everything they had promised.

Elroy planned the honeymoon; he just said to pack for a warm climate. When I woke up on my wedding day, I had no idea where we would be honeymooning.

But just as on Christmas morning in 2010, he surprised me once again. At the end of the reception, he announced that we would be going to St. Thomas in the Virgin Islands.

I'd come a long way from becoming Dr. Samantha Rogers in 2009. I was on track professionally and had found the right man after years of dating. That magic chemistry had happened, and we'd married as a result of a dating ad placed on a national website. But if I were to live the life I'd always envisioned, something was still missing: a baby. It was just one part of a much bigger picture, but for me it represented the culmination of my dreams, of the life I'd always seen in my mind whenever I looked into the future. For me, a family meant children, although I realized that this wasn't the case for every woman. I'd grown up surrounded by family and children, and I knew that I, too, had a lot to offer as a parent. Elroy and I were both successful and living comfortable lives. We had a solid relationship and it was time for the picture to be completed.

I assumed that nature would take its course and that I'd get pregnant. That's what happens, right? A couple marries and before too long a baby comes along. For me, however, having children wasn't going to be that easy. I didn't know it at the time, but enormous challenges lay ahead, ones that I couldn't have foreseen.

Summary and Points to Remember

I had gotten my doctorate and was ready to take the next steps in my life. Earning my degrees had involved taking the right steps in the right order. If you want an education (or a *higher* education), you fill out the applications, go to classes, study, and walk across the stage. Educational institutions have a familiar structure, and anyone who wants to pursue higher learning knows how to go about it. That doesn't mean that hard work isn't entailed or that difficulties aren't encountered. Indeed, my own position within the educational system is designed to help those who are struggling. But my point is that everyone knows that you go to school in order to learn and get a degree.

However, finding the right mate—that *soul* mate—with whom to settle down isn't as easy as it used to be. There's no established path as there is in education. Decades ago, people met through family or friends or when attending high school or college. Baby Boomer women started the trend of working outside the home and placed a great emphasis on their careers, with some foregoing motherhood altogether or raising children as single moms. In the twenty-first century, this paradigm shift has continued to even more complex models of family life. The population is larger and people move frequently to further their careers, with Millennials and Generation X waiting longer to get married and start families. The reasons they do so are fairly obvious: they want to establish their careers, find the right partner (they're not as quick to settle down, but instead date longer), and become financially stable. Most young adults in these categories end up having at least two children in the long run, but many do so in their mid to late thirties, and more than a few need fertility treatments (which we'll discuss later) in order to conceive.

Furthermore, with changing lifestyles and demographics, more and more people have turned to online dating and while there are some happy endings thanks to the internet, it's not a given. A great many people get frustrated with online dating which can be a minefield since online dating profiles can be filled with inaccuracies, outright lies, and out-of-date pictures. It's a paradox, really, since people now have access to an almost unlimited number of eligible men and women thanks to the digital age. Yet, online dating often seems to be a harder way to meet that perfect someone than more traditional ways that pre-date personal computers.

I was fortunate to meet Elroy, a man who was just the kind of husband I'd always wanted. I firmly believe that our meeting was directed by the hand of God, but I'd had to wait. When we pray or hope for something, we have to step back and let God answer in his own time. His timetable is always the right one.

Here are things I want you to remember regarding pursuing your career, delaying marriage, and dating in the twenty-first century.

- You don't have to choose between marriage and getting an education in order to become financially secure. Delaying marriage is the rule and not the exception in the twenty-first century.
- It's easier to get advanced degrees *before* you settle down with a life partner or have children. Working a fulltime job while going to graduate school can be daunting when trying to be present for your spouse and children. If your educational degrees are behind you and you've attained financial stability, you may be able to focus better on goals, such as finding a husband or planning a family. It varies from individual to individual, but time management and commitment may be easier once you've checked off the more basic steps that lead to the life you want to live.

- You've got to be proactive in finding a life partner or husband. You may meet your perfect match at a party and not have to expend a lot of effort.
- Online dating is one of many ways to find a spouse, but it takes patience. Don't be afraid to try it, but always be careful and don't be in a hurry to commit. Remember to always begin by meeting in public places to ensure safety.
- There are many books on dating and finding the perfect mate. Many are excellent, but don't be a slave to every how-to book on the subject. Finding a husband or wife isn't always about a series of steps or connecting the dots.
- When you meet someone you like, be patient. It took Elroy and me four months to really connect. One needs to exercise judgment, but keep an open mind as you proceed.
- Remember that there are other ways of meeting people. You may find a suitable partner in a meet-up group, a continuing education class, through a friend, or just about anywhere. Be open. God can help two people connect in the most unusual ways. I found Elroy online, but not on a dating site. Never try to limit what God can do.
- Expect a good outcome. If you believe that it's never going to happen for you, it probably won't.
- Never give up!

CHAPTER THREE

When Are You Going to Have a Baby?

It was time for a baby, but I thought that it would happen naturally, just as it was happening for so many people Elroy and I knew. As I've stated, it was my goal, but it wasn't one on which I thought I had to intentionally concentrate. I guess I expected to miss my period one day and then tell Elroy the good news, followed by a general announcement to family and friends. I'd go to the doctor for prenatal care and then have a baby. It would be a joyful time and we'd continue on with our lives, raising our son or daughter while pursuing all the things life had to offer.

Throughout the fall of 2011, we didn't take any kind of extraordinary measures to conceive since we didn't think they were necessary. When I didn't become pregnant, I thought to myself that maybe it would take a little bit longer for us. It wasn't unprecedented, so there was no reason to panic. I continued to pray and was sure God was going to answer my request.

We went to a funeral in Alabama in January of 2012, and my aunt's friend asked me when I was going to have a baby. I told her that we were ready and we discussed the issue of having children later in life. She was very encouraging, citing that she had given birth to her first child when she was forty-two. This was heartening since I was only thirty-six. Since Elroy and I were newlyweds, it was natural for people to ask the same question everywhere we went: Are you going to have kids? By springtime, Elroy and I turned thirty-seven in April and May, respectively. There was still no announcement to be made, and I thought I would bring up the subject at my annual OB/GYN exam in the summer.

When I saw my gynecologist, Dr. Sunny, we discussed my goal to have children. He stated that if I had not conceived by the following summer, then I would be considered medically infertile. He told me that I should download an app to track my time of ovulation, which occurred in the middle of a woman's menstrual cycle, to make sure that we were having sex at the right time of the month. In other words, we had to be more intentional in our effort to conceive. At the end of a year, he said he would prescribe fertility drugs if I were not yet pregnant. I wasn't interested in taking medication to help conceive because I didn't want to become an "octomom" since fertility drugs can cause multiple births.

To be on the safe side, and because I wanted to avoid taking these drugs if at all possible, I started to research ways to improve fertility in the summer of 2012. The literature stated that getting pregnant was more than just making love at the right time of the month. I'd been getting acupuncture, acupressure, and reflexology massages at the mall because they were relaxing, but I came across articles that said these treatments could also enhance fertility. In the fall of 2012, I continued to get reflexology and acupressure massages since the literature said that stimulating certain neural pathways in the body would increase the chances that I would conceive. These methods, at one time considered to be very much on the fringe of medicine, had become more accepted in mainstream society and I had no hesitation in trying them. Maybe, I thought, my body just needed a little extra help because of my age.

My biological clock was ticking much louder now and friends, family, and co-workers were asking constantly if and when we were going to have a baby. It was like listening to a mantra from whomever we met. People also had endless advice on what I should do. That wasn't unusual since people have recommended folk remedies to women for generations: drink pure spring water, eat more carrots, become a vegetarian, have a shot of whiskey before bed, drink buttermilk, and so forth. For me, the words I kept hearing were "just relax." Over and over again, the words kept coming: *Relax, relax, relax. Don't worry. It'll happen. You're trying too hard.* Ironically, they were telling me exactly what I'd started out doing from the very beginning of my marriage: not worry and assume that pregnancy would occur one day without any conscious effort.

I missed my period in January 2013, and felt different physically and emotionally. It's probably something only women can describe, and it was a case of, *I feel something different about my body and I believe I know the cause.* Could this be the moment I'd been waiting for? I went to the drugstore to buy an over-the-counter pregnancy kit. I urinated on the plastic stick that came with the kit and two blue lines appeared. I was pregnant! It had indeed taken a little longer than expected, but Elroy and I were elated and felt sure that everything would work out fine. I knew from the time elapsed since my last period that I'd gotten pregnant the previous December. I'd seen my mother on New Year's Day, and with motherly intuition she said I was glowing. "Are you pregnant?" she asked. I said I wasn't since I didn't want everyone to get excited before I knew for sure, but my gut feelings had been correct.

I made a doctor's appointment for my first prenatal appointment with Dr. Sunny after receiving a BFP—a Big Fat Positive—on my home pregnancy test. I was seven weeks along, and Elroy and I agreed not to tell anyone for three months since most miscarriages happen during the first trimester. For this reason, many couples elect to withhold the good news until the second trimester begins. What could be worse than making an announcement to dozens of friends, with word of mouth spreading to even more people, if things didn't work out?

We had planned to go to the Superbowl in New Orleans on February 3, 2013, and saw no reason to change our itinerary. We weren't going to the game but wanted to be in the city to soak up the ambience and festivities surrounding the event. I knew that getting a hurricane on Bourbon Street was out of the question since the famous French Quarter thoroughfare can get a little rowdy, and women are usually advised not to drink during pregnancy anyway. However, we would be able to go out to dinner and see the game at a sports bar and share in the excitement as the Ravens battled the 49ers. We had a great time and returned on Monday. I was not experiencing any nausea and had no reason to be concerned.

When I woke up on Tuesday morning to get dressed and go to work, I noticed a red spot in my underwear. Spotting, as it's known, is not uncommon during pregnancy, but it can also be an early sign of an impending miscarriage. I called my doctor's office and reported the symptom. The nurse stated that if the bleeding got worse that I should come in. I Googled "bleeding and pregnancy" to be as informed as I could, and the search results reinforced that spotting was common for many pregnant women regardless of their age.

I felt fine, so I went into work. When I used the restroom, I saw more blood, along with some clots. I felt certain that I was miscarrying. I needed to get to

Grady Memorial Hospital, the largest in Atlanta. Both Elroy and my co-worker, Stacey, offered to drive me, but I thought it would be quicker to drive myself, which I did.

Arriving at the ER, I was taken to triage immediately after showing my insurance card. I was hopeful that the worst might not happen, that maybe I'd arrived in time, and the ER doctor performed a cursory exam and drew my blood. My mother called me at Grady and said that she could be there in an hour, but I told her not to come, still harboring hope. The doctor returned and reassured me that I was indeed pregnant according to preliminary tests.

The next step was to get an ultrasound. During the procedure, the doctor said she couldn't see the amniotic sac and that I had probably miscarried. She didn't give me a definitive answer, only that I'd "probably" miscarried. I was to go home and schedule a follow-up appointment with my doctor. As much as I wanted to believe that there was still a glimmer of hope, I knew in my heart that I'd lost the baby. Three days later, it was confirmed that I'd miscarried. My HCG level was low. HCG stands for Human Chorionic Gonadotropin, a hormone that spikes when a woman becomes pregnant and is detectable in blood and urine. Days later, mine had shown a marked decrease.

I had some very dark days in the weeks following the miscarriage. I was devastated since Elroy and I had wanted a child so badly. I was thirty-seven years old and wasn't sure whether I'd ever be able to get pregnant again, and even if I could, would I be able to carry the baby to term? I cried often, prayed, and asked God "Why me?" Hadn't I been a faithful servant? Wasn't I living a good life, working hard, and attending church? It seemed as if everybody around me was having children, so why couldn't I? Would the last component of the life I'd dreamed of for so long going to be denied me forever? I experienced the stages of grief: shock, pain, guilt (blaming myself for being infertile), anger, bargaining, depression, encouragement that things might yet turn out okay, renewing my mindset, and accepting my situation with the resolution that I would try to conceive again. I've listed the stages, but actually going through them was a long and painful ordeal as I searched for a light at the end of the tunnel.

Happily, this wasn't the end of my story, as you'll see in the next several chapters. There was a silver lining to the cloud that hung over me, and I realized that my hope of having a child had not evaporated.

Summary and Points to Remember

I learned that even though my biological clock was ticking as I moved into my late thirties, I was still able to get pregnant. As noted earlier, more and more people are waiting to have children, and moving past age thirty-five doesn't mean that things are hopeless. Many women in this age bracket conceive and have successful outcomes. It should be noted for the sake of completeness, however, that pregnancy after thirty-five is not without risks, and these are worth mentioning so that you can discuss them with your healthcare provider.

A woman is born with a certain number of eggs, with an egg being released fourteen days before a menstrual cycle. As women age, they have fewer eggs and the eggs they still have as they move into their thirties and forties are older and are not as easily fertilized by male sperm. Put simply, it can be harder to get pregnant after thirty-five. Also, older eggs may not be genetically sound and this increases the chances of a child having birth defects, including Down syndrome, autism, or other disorders. Additionally, a woman over thirty-five is at greater risk for premature birth, giving birth to a child with low birth weight, giving birth to multiples (twins, triplets, or many more), and stillbirth.

Women over thirty-five may also have complications during pregnancy due to pre-existing diabetes, hypertension (high blood pressure), and preeclampsia. The latter is a condition in which a woman's liver and kidneys are compromised in the second trimester. The condition is usually identified by high protein levels in the urine, headaches, and vision disturbances.

I want to strongly emphasize that these risk factors do not mean that women should avoid getting pregnant just because they're in their thirties. Many of the above medical conditions can affect much younger women as well. Also, keep in mind that in generations past when people had large families, it was common for women to give birth to as many as ten children (or more) over a period of twenty years, taking them into their forties, and they did so at a time when medicine was not nearly as sophisticated as it is today. I'm simply saying that women should be well-informed so as to make the best decisions for themselves in conjunction with their doctors. In Chapter Two, I listed the benefits of electing to delay having children, so there are pros and cons to take into account when you discuss the matter with your partner and physician.

Another risk of having children later in life is a higher incidence of miscarriage. It happened to me and it was devastating. I blamed myself and coped with the stages of grief, but I learned that I could get through it and that it wasn't the end of the world—or my quest to have a baby. I also had the support of my husband and our relationship deepened as a result of the experience. Sometimes the greatest victories grow from defeats that seem overwhelming—but don't have to be in the long run. I knew God hadn't abandoned me. If I were in his hands, then I could eventually take a deep breath and move on with my life. To paraphrase St. Paul's words in 2 Corinthians 12:9, God is strongest when we ourselves are weak.

Here are the main points I want you to take to heart from my experiences described in this chapter.

- Having a baby later in life is sometimes (though not always) harder, and it may take you longer to get pregnant.
- You should be aware of the risks involved when getting pregnant over the age of thirty-five.
- Always consult an OB/GYN physician when considering getting pregnant or if you discover that you are already pregnant. This holds true for women at any age but is all the more important if you are in your thirties, especially over thirty-five.
- Reduce your stress in order to stay healthy and lessen the risk factors mentioned above.
- Avoid smoking, drugs, and alcohol.
- If you suffer a miscarriage, get medical help as soon as possible and keep all follow-up appointments.
- A miscarriage does not necessarily mean that all hope is lost for getting pregnant again. To the contrary, it's often a positive sign that you *are* able to get pregnant, although this may not be true for all women depending on more complicated medical conditions.
- Share your feelings with your spouse or partner, and let him express his as well. Remember that the miscarriage represents a loss for both of you.
- Allow your partner to take care of you.
- Discuss future goals with your partner regarding the possibility of getting pregnant again. Don't give up your dream because of one failed attempt. Some women have several miscarriages but go on to have healthy children.
- Adopt the mindset that obstacles are meant to be overcome. If you find yourself slipping into depression, get help as soon as possible from

a qualified mental healthcare provider. If you don't know of one, your gynecologist or primary care physician will be happy to give you a referral.

• Trust in God and make daily time for prayer and reflection. Don't be afraid to tell God what you want or how you're feeling. When you're finished praying, leave the matter in his hands and have faith. He can see the big picture and knows what you're going through. Find peace in his presence and love.

CHAPTER FOUR

Doctors... and More Doctors

I went for a follow-up visit with my gynecologist, Dr. Sunny, who actually celebrated my miscarriage. He asserted that my fallopian tubes were open and that because I'd gotten pregnant once, I could conceive again since there was no underlying medical condition preventing me from doing so. As he put it, "I had an opening!" He was referring to the condition of my reproductive system, not his office schedule, and I was ecstatic that a new light had dawned in my life. My dream hadn't died, and I tried to frame the miscarriage in positive terms. I'd been able to get pregnant naturally, plus the miscarriage had occurred very early on in my pregnancy so that I hadn't invested as much attachment to the unborn child as I would have if I'd been six or seven months into the pregnancy. I would be able to make a fresh start without a great deal of waiting and the new hope I now had lifted my spirits and gave me the extra motivation I needed to move on from the tragedy.

My taxman asked when we were having children. I shared with him my struggles to have a baby and he advised me to give the baby a name and talk to him. He advocated that I literally speak the baby into existence. I took his advice. Elroy and I had already chosen a boy's name, which was James Colin, and I began talking to my womb, saying, "James, come on!" Also, Pamela, one of my co-workers, had previously told me to write down affirmations about getting married and having children and carry them around in my wallet. She said that when I finally had a child, she and her husband would babysit for me. Other co-workers, Rosa, Naomi and Dwight were always encouraging. Dwight was inspiring because he and his wife had seven children.

My friends from work Carol, Diana, Josephine, and Tracey would often say specific prayers to bless and open my womb after the miscarriage. Jesus said that where two or more are gathered in his name, he is in their midst and will grant their prayers (Matthew 18:20). This is a powerful scriptural passage and I wanted to practice its message.

With this mindset, Elroy and I were able to carry on with our lives. In the spring of 2013, Elroy and I traveled to Hilton Head, South Carolina, and in June, we attended our twentieth year high school reunions in Enterprise and Littleton. At my tenth high school reunion, I told myself that I wouldn't return unless I was married. At my twentieth, I boldly claimed that I wouldn't return unless I was pregnant or had children. Strangely enough, the subject of when we were going to have kids never came up.

Elroy and I turned thirty-eight—I wasn't upset that another twelve pages had been turned on the calendar without a baby in the home—and I played kickball in a league that summer. We were happy, on the go, and remembered that we needed to try to be intentional in our effort to conceive, as Dr. Sunny had put it. It was no longer a question of "when it happens, it happens." We knew that, at the very least, mindfulness of our objective was important if I were going to get pregnant again. That having been said, I was still optimistic since Dr. Sunny had been so enthusiastic after the miscarriage. I'd learned one very important fact: there was nothing wrong with "the equipment."

My confidence didn't mean that I wasn't going to be proactive as we tried. I decided that acupuncture and reflexology might be in order again. Women who undergo acupuncture have higher rates of pregnancy and live births. Acupuncture, of course, is the ancient Chinese art of inserting sterilized stainless steel needles into certain points of the human body called meridians, which are thought to be channels of energy. It is believed that such treatments can lower stress by decreasing the stress hormone progesterone (Karras, n.d.). More generally, acupuncture calms the nervous system, helps the body repair itself at the cellular level, and increases blood flow to various parts of the body. In the case of women, treatments can increase the blood flow to the uterus. Elroy commented good-naturedly that I was a glutton for needles.

Reflexology is a form of acupressure that entails massaging points on the feet that correspond to various organs throughout the entire body, thus releasing energy that the Chinese call *chi*. The technique is strongly related to the theory behind acupuncture in that reflexology supposedly releases healing energies throughout the body by applying a stimulus to critical points on the exterior of the body. Reflexology is also meant to restore balance to the mind-body connection and is, therefore, a popular holistic treatment that has gained mainstream acceptance over the last thirty years. As Karen Hawthorn points out in her article *The Unquantifiable Benefits of Reflexology for Fertility*, reflexology can stimulate the body's electrical energy and blood flow to the ovaries and uterus, as well as the immune, circulatory, and endocrine systems (Hawthorn, 2015). More specifically, reflexology can stimulate the liver and kidneys to increase the libido and balance hormone levels related to conception.

But I wasn't finished with holistic measures yet. I was off for the summer so in July I consulted Dr. Ramirez, a medical doctor at the Preventative Medicine Clinic. Dr. Ramirez, who ran the clinic with other doctors, was a believer in holistic approaches to health within mainstream medicine, and he offered nutritional counseling augmented by vitamin injections. I was looking at my body and overall health the way one might look at an automobile: machinery needs maintenance and repair. If my body was older than those of most women who got pregnant, then I needed to get into optimal shape in the same way that one might get a tune-up for an automobile. My research had shown that all parts of the body work together, and if I could get in shape and do everything that was humanly possible to be healthy, then I would maximize my chances of getting pregnant again by ensuring that all of my organ systems were working in harmony with each other. I discontinued the nutritional counseling with Dr. Ramirez after August since his treatments were expensive, but I'd at least taken another step towards my goal. As long as I was doing things to enhance my chances of having a child, I was avoiding worry that I might not experience the outcome I desired. Remaining idle is the best way for negative thinking and stress to creep into one's mind, so I remained active throughout the year.

All of the above didn't mean that I'd abandoned conventional medicine by any means. I went for my six-month check-up in August, but Dr. Sunny had left the practice by then. I spoke with a female doctor and shared with her that Dr. Sunny had previously discussed prescribing fertility medications and might even have referred me to a fertility specialist. The new doctor prescribed my first round of a drug called Clomid.

Clomid, the brand name for the generic Clomifene, is used to help treat women who have fertility issues because they may ovulate irregularly or release no eggs at all as they get older. This is common among women in any age bracket who have irregular menstrual cycles, which was the case with me. Many times, women are given Clomid because they have Polycystic Ovarian Syndrome (PCOS). This disorder is characterized by the irregular release of eggs or small cysts on the ovaries. I was somewhat reluctant to take the drug since I was still concerned that I might be subject to multiple births (as before, I was afraid of becoming the next octomom), but I couldn't neglect conventional medical treatment, and I was going to use every tool at my disposal, both holistic and conventional.

Elroy and I continued to follow sports in the fall. We were Falcons season ticket holders for home games and also attended Atlanta Braves games. We also traveled to Elroy's homecoming at North Carolina AT&T State University in Greensboro, North Carolina. Sports had been a big part of our courtship, and it remained a part of our marriage.

September was our second wedding anniversary and we went to Washington, DC. We also went to the baby shower for one of Elroy's friends in nearby Maryland. My heart ached for my husband since all of his friends had children— some even had grandchildren—and there I was, struggling to conceive. As I looked around the reception room, I blamed myself and thought that maybe it would have been better for him if he'd married someone younger, someone who was fertile and wouldn't have had trouble giving him a child. Like most men, he wanted a son. But I recalled our wedding vows that we would care for each other through sickness and health. I also realized that I wasn't giving Elroy enough credit for his understanding and patience. He may have been frustrated, but he was very supportive of my efforts and stated that we still had plenty of time. He reminded me of the lady that we'd met at the funeral in 2012, the one who'd had her first baby at the age of forty-two. I put away my doubt and self-pity quickly. After two years of marriage, I hadn't hit my goal exactly on the mark of having my first child by thirty-eight (I'd pushed it up from forty after the wedding), but was I throwing in the towel? The thought didn't enter my mind.

It's important to note that adoption did come up during this time, although I'd entertained the idea of foster parenting years earlier if I failed to get married. Now that I was married to Elroy, we discussed adoption. Adoption can certainly be a wonderful thing, however we wanted to keep trying to conceive. I felt in my heart that I could indeed get pregnant. My dream had always been to have my very own child, and I was still holding tenaciously to it. Elroy was right. There was still time.

But I wasn't pregnant despite being on Clomid. Since Dr. Sunny had left the practice, I decided to find a new OB/GYN, someone who was a fertility specialist. Dr. Hastings was a renowned physician who had been honored by his peers and even the Congress of the United States, which had bestowed upon him the National Senatorial Medal of Freedom for his efforts in advocating healthcare reform so that everyone in the United States would have 100 percent coverage. He also specialized in gynecological surgery and the reversal of tubal ligations, which is commonly called "getting your tubes tied." His specialization in the overall area of fertility made him my logical choice. I felt as if I were going to the "best of the best."

I spoke with Dr. Hastings for the first time on October 11, 2013. We discussed my miscarriage and my goal to become pregnant again. He prescribed a second round of Clomid and told me to use ovulation kits. The average over-the-counter ovulation kit is designed to tell a couple the best time in a woman's cycle to have intercourse by monitoring the presence of luteinizing hormone in her urine. This hormone increases one to two days before a woman ovulates. The test is performed at any time of day, although some kits instruct the woman to test in the morning. It is generally advisable to start testing when a build-up of cervical mucus is detected as this is also a harbinger that ovulation is about to commence. The kits don't always work for several reasons. Many women experiencing fertility issues have irregular periods or their bodies don't release eggs during their cycles, a condition called anovulation. My menstrual cycles were still irregular, and perhaps for that reason the ovulation kits didn't work for me.

By late October, Dr. Hastings performed a hysterosalpingogram, or HSG, on me. This is a very painful procedure in which a contrast dye is injected into a thin tube that is inserted through the vagina and into the uterus. The object of the exam is to take radiological pictures of the uterus and fallopian tubes to ascertain whether there is any blockage that would prevent the egg from passing cleanly though the tube or, by the same token, preventing the man's sperm ascending the tube to fertilize the egg. At times, the dye can actually open a blocked tube, rendering the test curative in nature. The HSG also looks for irregularities in the uterus, such as infection, polyps, fibroid tumors, adhesions, or foreign objects (Hysterosalpingogram, 2012).

In my case, none of these abnormalities was detected—no biological or structural defect was found that indicated I couldn't get pregnant—and that was good news indeed. Dr. Hastings continued his aggressive approach by checking Elroy's sperm for motility, or as it's commonly referred to, their ability to swim. Elroy dutifully made his deposit and the test came back negative, meaning that his sample had been completely normal.

By November, I still wasn't pregnant, so Dr. Hastings gave me an ultrasound, a new course of Clomid, and an injection of HCG, the hormone previously mentioned that is associated with pregnancy. Like luteinizing hormone, it can trigger ovulation, usually within thirty-eight to forty hours after the injection. This was done in conjunction with artificial insemination, technically known as intrauterine insemination or IUI. You might say that Dr. Hastings was throwing everything in his fertility arsenal at my problem. The out-of-pocket costs of IUI and HSG were very high, although money would be secondary if these procedures resulted in a viable pregnancy.

Intrauterine insemination is used to increase the number of sperm that will reach the fallopian tubes—giving Mother Nature a little help you might say, by placing the sperm as close as possible to the egg descending from the ovaries. Elroy's sperm had tested normal, but we chose to take the helping hand since Dr. Hastings thought it might do the trick. The procedure is usually performed after medication is administered to stimulate ovulation—think of this entire approach as a one-two punch. It is also timed to coincide with the increase of luteinizing hormone, meaning that the sperm is deposited in the woman's body about twenty-four to thirty-six hours after the hormonal increase (Intrauterine Insemination: IUI, 2017). A catheter is used for the actual insertion of the sperm into the uterus after the sperm has been separated from the man's seminal fluid.

By December, I wasn't pregnant. I was frustrated but not defeated. I hadn't come this far to give up, and I still felt deep in my soul that a pregnancy was meant to be. This may not sound logical, but I trusted in both God and my own instincts. My dream had been formed in childhood, and it had taken root to the extent that I was convinced that—somehow, some way—I would have a child. A second IUI was scheduled for January of 2014 in conjunction with taking two more medications, Menopur and Femera, costing over $400 for the medication alone.

These drugs are used when Clomid has had no effect in fertility treatment. Both drugs contain Follicle Stimulating Hormones (FSH) that stimulate follicles in the ovaries to release eggs. Menopur also contains luteinizing hormone. Also, both drugs can cause multiple eggs to be released during a single ovulation cycle, thus increasing the possibility of multiple fertilizations and births. The common attribute of all the drugs I've mentioned is that they are meant to stimulate ovulation through hormonal therapy, whether they are hormones themselves or stimulate the body's own natural hormones to be secreted. As mentioned, this was the reason I was hesitant to begin any kind of fertility drug treatment at all but the medications now seemed called for, so I decided to give it another try.

I took the medications, stayed positive, and prayed. It was a team effort, with God, Elroy, Dr. Hastings, and me on the team. Time would tell, but as far as I was concerned, I was going to have a baby.

Summary and Points to Remember

Elroy and I were getting older, and at times I grew frustrated. Nevertheless, I pressed forward; I tried holistic approaches, but with my eye on the calendar as I entered my late thirties, I decided to try methods prescribed by conventional medicine. It was costly and time-consuming, but the other option was to do nothing at all. Fertility drugs had helped tens of thousands of women, some of them older, to conceive and give birth to healthy babies.

In the Gospel of Luke, Jesus told this parable: "Suppose you have a friend, and you go to him at midnight and say, 'Friend, lend me three loaves of bread; a friend of mine on a journey has come to me, and I have no food to offer him.' And suppose the one inside answers, 'Don't bother me. The door is already locked, and my children and I are in bed. I can't get up and give you anything.' I tell you, even though he will not get up and give you the bread because of friendship, yet because of your shameless audacity he will surely get up and give you as much as you need" (Luke 11: 5-8).

Persistence is the key to having so many of our prayers answered. God knew what I wanted; and there was no reason I could think of as to why he wouldn't want me to have a child. If God wanted me to keep knocking, that's what I would do. Ultimately, my answer resided with him. Maybe the right approach was holistic, traditional, or something I hadn't encountered yet. Regardless, the answer was out there.

Here are the points from this chapter I want you to remember:

- Don't be afraid to explore holistic approaches. I chose acupuncture, accupressure, and reflexology, but you may come across other literature that resonates with your own body and thinking. Some people try aromatherapy, music that inspires them, conventional massage, hypnotherapy, or methods (some of which may sound a bit silly) that have been passed down for generations in their families. As long as they seem sound and you're not violating safe medical practices, consider the alternatives. Be very careful, however, when taking herbal supplements since some can be highly toxic and can harm both mother and fetus should conception occur.

- Alternative approaches have been used successfully for years, long before the advent of modern medicine. Just make sure that your individual approach poses no threat to your health. Some folk remedies are based in fact, while others are not and may be dangerous.

- The importance of nutrition cannot be overrated. Quite literally, we are what we eat, and almost any endeavor in life can be enhanced by eating a healthy diet. This is doubly true for women of any age who wish to get pregnant, especially those who are older. What we eat impacts every cell, tissue, and organ in our bodies. People are aware that eating certain foods can be either beneficial or harmful (to their hearts, for example). The same holds true for a woman's reproductive system. But remember that the reproductive system doesn't function in isolation. Aim for bringing optimal health to your entire body.

- Don't neglect the mind-body connection or underestimate the power of positive thinking. Every thought we have impacts the cells of our bodies and our metabolism. Angry, negative, or stressful thoughts can cause our brains to send thousands of harmful chemicals throughout our bodies, including adrenaline and cortisol, also known as "fight or flight" chemicals. The chemicals produced by negative thoughts can impact health even at the level of our DNA. On the other hand, positive thoughts send healthy chemicals throughout the body that can repair, restore, and energize our bodies and our health. These concepts are no longer considered to be on the fringe of mainstream medicine. They are accepted as fact by medical science.

- If you're having trouble conceiving after regular trips to your OB/GYN doctor, consider finding a fertility specialist. You may discover someone by word of mouth or an online search, but fertility is a major branch of gynecology, and specialists abound across the country. A consultation will not obligate you to follow any course of action, but you'll learn what your options are. If your biological clock is ticking, don't squander valuable time. Get a professional medical opinion.

- While certain risks are attached to taking fertility drugs, your doctor or fertility specialist knows your overall health and can tell you if the possible benefits outweigh the risks. Remember that millions of women successfully conceive after taking the medications (and others) that I've mentioned in this chapter.

- Consider intrauterine insemination if your doctor believes that the procedure might help you and your partner have a child. The procedure has been around for many years, and while it isn't guaranteed to result in conception, it has helped many women have children, especially when used in conjunction with fertility drugs.

- Learn about your body and ovulation so that you can understand the female reproductive process, as well as the process of ovulation. Without this important knowledge, many of the methods and procedures discussed in this chapter may seem unnecessarily confusing. Even if you aren't using expensive fertility treatments, you need to understand the basics of ovulation so that you know the optimal times of the month to engage in sexual intercourse.

- If you're an older woman, consider using an integrated approach to getting pregnant, using both standard medical procedures and alternative or holistic treatments as long as they do not work against each other. Always consult your physician to make sure that your integrated approach is medically safe.

- Pray every day and remember that a higher power is in control of our lives when we have the faith and boldness to place our desires and problems in God's hands. As St. Paul said in Ephesians 3:20, "Now to him who is able to do immeasurably more than all we ask or imagine, according to his power that is at work within us . . . ." Are you limiting yourself by limiting God? God made the world and all that is in it, and he knows the rhythms and cycles of his creation, which includes the rhythms of a woman's body. Give your concerns to God daily and then step back with peace of mind.

CHAPTER FIVE

Let Go and Let God

By the end of February 2014, drug therapy and another IUI procedure hadn't worked, so I decided to cease all medications and try to conceive naturally again. The medications and procedures had been very costly out of pocket, and while I had no problem paying such high prices to obtain positive results, pregnancy hadn't occurred. I wasn't giving up, just moving back in the direction of trying a natural approach.

My first step was to buy the OvaCue Fertility Monitor. The monitor was much different than the traditional ovulation kits I'd used. The OvaCue registers changes in a woman's electrolyte levels by simply inserting the monitor onto one's tongue, which thankfully meant no more urinating on a stick. The monitor marks the fertility period for a woman by providing indicators, rendered in various shades of blue, five to seven days prior to ovulation. Couples are expected to have intercourse on these "blue days" to increase the chances of pregnancy. The monitor costs $400, but it's both sophisticated and simple to use, plus it keeps daily track of readings and compares them to readings from the previous month. In this respect, the monitor is ideal for women whose menstrual cycles are irregular or those who may have Polycystic Ovarian Syndrome. Other ovulation kits are designed only to reflect the levels of estrogen and luteinizing hormone in a woman's body. OvaCue uses a different system that makes each monitor sensitive to a particular individual's electrolyte levels (Fertility Monitors Can Reduce the Time It Takes to Conceive, 2017).

Next, I began treatments with Dr. Leaf, a licensed bio-energy practitioner, at an acupuncture clinic in Atlanta, a center that offered many holistic treatments for a variety of disorders. Dr. Leaf was a fertility specialist in addition to being a bio-energy practitioner. She was very positive and encouraging. She said that I was going to get pregnant and that she'd had great success with other patients who had the same goal. In addition to acupuncture treatments, she prescribed wheat germ oil. The oil contained carbohydrates, protein, fats, vitamins, and minerals to help the body store the necessary energy it takes to conceive. Undergoing these treatments was far easier than taking numerous fertility medications, receiving injections, and undergoing intrauterine insemination. In fact, as I already noted, they were relaxing. From February through May, I received ten acupuncture treatments from Dr. Leaf, each costing $85. School ended on May 31, and I still wasn't pregnant. I received four more treatments that ended in July, but I still wasn't seeing any results.

During the summer, Elroy and I went on a cruise to the Bahamas and we also got our season tickets for Falcons games, ready again for football. Our love of travel and sports hadn't been diminished by the issue of fertility, but I nevertheless held on to many scriptural passages in addition to the ones already mentioned.

I decided that it was time to focus more on prayer. In early fall I heard a sermon that really spoke to my spirit. Dr. Kelvin Teamer, minister at the Bouldercrest Church of Christ, delivered the sermon and one of its themes was "Let Go and Let God." I'd been praying, but I thought that maybe faith needed more emphasis in my personal life. The sermon was about understanding the true nature of meekness. The modern connotation of the word "meek" is one of submissiveness. People who are meek are considered to be docile and deficient in courage and strength. Meekness is equated with weakness. When Jesus exhorted his followers to be meek, however, he wanted them to be gentle and humble, and that definition doesn't tally with our modern use of the term. Instead, Dr. Teamer pointed out that meekness was strength under control. In Matthew 11:28-29, Jesus said, "Come to me, all you who are weary and burdened, and I will give you rest. Take my yoke upon you and learn from me, for I am gentle and humble in heart, and you will find rest for your souls." Jesus was certainly not a weak person. He performed great miracles by healing people of disease and cured lepers, the blind, deaf, paralyzed, and those with all sorts of physical afflictions. This demonstrated strength, not weakness. In exhorting us to be meek, Jesus was instructing us not to boast or be prideful, but constantly told his disciples to have faith strong enough to move mountains. Mountain-moving faith is a sign of great confidence and strength, not a lack of courage.

Finally, Dr. Teamer discussed James 4:10, which says, "Humble yourselves before the Lord, and he will lift you up." But what did that mean? How does one humble herself before God? The answer is that you hand your prayers confidently over to God. In other words, you let go (you humble yourself) and let God (allow his power to work in your life through faith). God promises great blessings to those who are meek enough to "let go and let God." It takes a humble spirit to walk into the abundant blessings that God wishes to grant us.

The sermon resonated with me deeply, and I realized yet again that God was in control but I had to allow him to take that role. Jesus said that, "Truly I tell you, if you have faith as small as a mustard seed, you can say to this mountain, 'Move from here to there,' and it will move. Nothing will be impossible for you" (Matthew 17:20). I thought deeply about those words. Mountains could really move! Nothing would be impossible! It wasn't about a *lack* of strength but rather about having *more* strength as long as we have a corresponding attitude of humility. I bought several small pins that had mustard seeds inside of them and carried one in my purse at all times as a reminder of the awesome power of faith. God was all-powerful but I had to do my part as well. I had to have faith the size of a mustard seed.

There were other verses that I prayed as well, such as "Rejoice always, pray continually, give thanks in all circumstances; for this is God's will for you in Christ Jesus" (1 Thessalonians 5:16-18); "Now faith is confidence in what we hope for and assurance about what we do not see" (Hebrews 11:1); "Ask and it will be given to you; seek and you will find; knock and the door will be opened to you" (Matthew 7:7); "Come near to God and he will come near to you. Wash your hands, you sinners, and purify your hearts, you double-minded" (James 4:8); "Do not conform to the pattern of this world, but be transformed by the renewing of your mind. Then you will be able to test and approve what God's will is—his good, pleasing and perfect will" (Romans 12:2).

That's exactly what I was doing: renewing my mind by immersing myself in these scriptural passages in order to strengthen my faith. The concepts common to all of these passages and to Dr. Teamer's sermon were strength, power, and faith. Prayer is an ally when used intelligently and properly, and I was going to try to move the biggest mountain in my life: infertility. Some might have easily said, "Well, it's not meant to be. God's will is that I be infertile," but that paints quite an unflattering portrait of our Creator. The Bible says that the Father in heaven gives good things to his children, and I didn't believe that God wished me to be infertile or deny my wish to have a child of my own.

I shared my continued goal with co-workers, Carol, and Diana since they knew about my miscarriage. One of my co-workers was especially encouraging since she'd had six healthy children even though she'd had a miscarriage, too. Another co-worker had given birth to two boys, with a miscarriage between their births. I shared bible verses with them, verses that spoke of overcoming infertility. There were so many examples of barren women in the Bible who the Lord touched and his power caused them to conceive.

Psalm 113 says, "He settles the childless woman in her home as a happy mother of children." In Genesis, God told Abraham, "Is anything too hard for the Lord? I will return to you at the appointed time next year, and Sarah will have a son" (Genesis 18:14). This quote refers to God's promise that he would multiply Abraham's descendants and cause them to become the great nation of Israel. It all began with his promise that Abraham's wife would bear him a son. Abraham was ninety-nine and his wife, Sarah, was approximately ten years younger when three angels appeared to Abraham and told him that his wife would conceive a son by the following year. Sarah did indeed give birth to a son, who was called Isaac.

There were many other instances in the Bible of women who were infertile but conceived with God's help. Rebecca and Rachel, the wives of Isaac and Jacob, respectively, were barren but bore healthy children. In the New Testament, Elizabeth and Zachariah were both up in years and beyond childbearing age, and yet Elizabeth gave birth to John the Baptist. Men who were infertile were also aided by God throughout the scriptures.

It is important to recall what God told Abraham: "Is anything too hard for the Lord?" If God can make an entire universe from nothing, can't he cause a woman to conceive? Of course he can! I recited these verses frequently, and Elroy and I prayed together.

Summary and Points to Remember

Medical procedures to boost fertility and initiate conception weren't working for me, so I decided again to try to get pregnant naturally although I realized that Elroy and I needed to try more intentionally. I was considered medically infertile, so I knew that I had to take certain measures to increase my chances of having a baby. For now, however, I'd done what I could by using the very latest methods that conventional medicine had to offer, and it was time to try a different approach. I returned to acupuncture and reflexology, although this time I used a licensed bio-energy practitioner that was well-versed in matters of infertility.

I also focused on my faith and did that, too, in an intentional manner. The sermon I'd heard on "Let Go and Let God" was particularly inspiring, and I also delved deeply into scripture, especially those passages that emphasized that God honored his promises and those that spoke of him curing infertility problems. I knew that the age of miracles hadn't passed, and if God could do it for others, then I knew he could do it for me as well. Scripture, after all, was there to inspire everybody for all times and places, not just a few people thousands of years ago. The words of the Bible are alive, living and breathing, and they spoke to me at this period of my life. "Let go and let God" wasn't a new phrase, but I thought it was time for me to take this advice more seriously. Sharing the verses with Elroy and my friends was also a source of encouragement and optimism.

Here is what I want you to remember about this chapter.

- When it comes to getting pregnant, it's not always a case either/or—of using only conventional medicine or only alternative approaches such as holistic medicine.
- The OvaCue is based on body chemistry related to electrolytes, hormones, and ovulation. The monitor tracks a woman's cycle very reliably and scientifically, and it's an important tool to use, especially if you have irregular periods or if traditional kits aren't working for you.
- Regardless of what approach you take towards that all-important goal of getting pregnant or having that first child later in life, I advise that you make God a part of your official plan. While many might regard this as a psychological trick of the mind that produces false hope or is a diversion that makes you feel better in the short term, I found it to be a genuine source of strength.
- If you are not currently a person of faith or prayer, it's never too late to give it a try.
- God can do all things. The Almighty Power who made the majestic stars and galaxies also made you and your body, and he certainly can touch you if you're open to receiving his help.

- The Bible teaches us that we can accomplish mighty goals by using faith as small as a mustard seed. If you're not perfect, remember that no one is. God wants to give you good things. It all starts with something as simple as a thought: "God, please help me conceive."
- Remember the many miracles and healings described in the Bible. Read about these wonders, reflect on them, and share them with friends. Faith can be infectious, and studies show that people who pray experience better mental and physical health. Prayer truly works.
- The Bible shows us that infertility was a common problem among women for thousands of years. More importantly, it shows that it's a hurdle you can overcome with God's help. He said, "Be fruitful and multiply." Having children is literally a part of his plan. Find scriptures about infertile women being helped by the Lord and you'll become more hopeful and expectant.
- If you don't think that your prayers are being answered, keep praying. Jesus taught his disciples to persevere in hardship and never give up.
- The Bible tells us not to worry and to "look at the birds of the air; they do not sow or reap or store away in barns, and yet your heavenly Father feeds them. Are you not much more valuable than they?" "Can any one of you by worrying add a single hour to your life?" (Matthew 6:25-34)
- The scriptures on fertility that I found most helpful are as follows: Genesis 18:9-15; Genesis 25:21; Genesis 29:30; Genesis 30:22-24; Judges 13:3-12; 1 Samuel 2:21; 2 Kings 4:8-17; and Luke 1:5-25.

CHAPTER SIX

New Procedures, New Options

I'd been filled with faith during the summer of 2014 and had received new encouragement from friends and colleagues. Even my professional life had been blessed. I'd begun a new position as Student Support Team and Response to Intervention Specialist (SST/RTI) that entailed identifying a student's academic weakness, determining what interventions are appropriate to address that weakness, and monitoring the student's progress with an eye to changing the intervention if necessary.

But I still hadn't gotten pregnant. I can understand how many women, especially those who are getting older, make the decision to walk away from the process—to give up their dream or else adopt a child. The process I was going through entailed an enormous amount of time and expense. You must recall from the early chapters of this book, however, that I am a goal-oriented person tenacious in pursuing what I want, and also naturally optimistic. Convinced through faith and prayer that nothing is impossible, I decided to move forward. I also had a special shield, which was an innate sense that God could not only work miracles, but that he was on my side, that he was prompting me to move forward, encouraging me to speak to the mountain of infertility and tell it to move.

Intrauterine insemination hadn't worked and neither had natural methods. Since neither was working, I decided it was now time to turn back to medicine again since there was another more expensive procedure I hadn't tried yet, one that has been used for several decades. I was walking a path of hope and trying to use every method at my disposal. You might say that I was metaphorically trying to pull down a baby from the heavens, and you wouldn't be far from wrong, but I was doing so because I was convinced that a baby was part of God's plan for my life. I'd always seen myself as being a wife and mother one day. It was this inward knowing that propelled me forward, not false hope.

For the first time I considered in vitro fertilization, known as IVF, which you might say is one step beyond artificial insemination. However, there was one problem—I didn't have the money to pay for the procedure. In IVF, mature eggs are harvested from a woman's ovaries and they're then fertilized in a medical laboratory with sperm from the woman's partner (or donor sperm if a woman is single or if her partner's sperm lacks motility). Only five percent of women with infertility issues use this method, but since 1981, over 200,000 babies have been born as a result of IVF (Infertility and In Vitro Fertilization, 2015). In vitro fertilization is used when there are problems with the uterus or fallopian tubes, ovulation, or an inability of the sperm to penetrate the cervical mucus secreted by a woman's body. Other times, it's used when all other attempts have failed even if the doctor can't put his finger on an exact reason as to why conception hasn't occurred. That was the category I fell into since, as stated, exams had shown my uterus and fallopian tubes were normal and healthy.

The actual procedure of harvesting eggs can be done in different ways. The basic method originally was to retrieve eggs from the uterus or fallopian tubes and then mix them with sperm in a sterile glass dish. Chances of pregnancy using this direct method are extremely low, however. It is now more common to stimulate the ovaries in order to get them to produce multiple eggs or to use a transvaginal ultrasound to take the eggs directly from the ovaries. Eggs are examined following their harvest to screen for viability and possible defects so that only healthy eggs are used in subsequent parts of the procedure. The eggs are also separated from any other cells surrounding them that may have become attached during the harvesting procedure. Before fertilization is attempted, a man's semen is "washed" to separate the active sperm from seminal fluid, which is fluid secreted by a man's prostate and seminal vesicles. It is the spermatozoa, the actual cells that penetrate an egg to trigger fertilization, which is used for IVF. By eliminating the other fluids, the actual spermatozoa have a better chance of finding and fertilizing an egg.

Once an embryo has been created through the processes described above, the embryos are rated using a scoring system to determine which are the most viable for transplantation to a woman's uterus. An embryo should contain two to four cells after forty-eight hours, and seven to ten cells after seventy-two hours. The embryos are also checked under a microscope for cell regularity and fragmentation. Regularity means that all of the observable cells are the same size (this is the norm), while fragmentation refers to whether or not any of the cells have broken away from the center of the embryo. It is desirable that no fragmentation be present (Sherbahn, 2017). Embryos are usually examined and scored forty-eight hours after fertilization has occurred.

Single women use sperm banks, but that's not part of my story since I was married and wanted a child with my husband. In even rarer cases, a surrogate known as a "gestational carrier" receives the fertilized eggs if the woman desiring to be a mother has a medical condition that would make it unsafe for her to undergo pregnancy in her own body. Again, that wasn't my goal. I wanted to carry my child myself.

Like other fertility treatments, in vitro fertilization carries risks. Because multiple eggs are fertilized, resulting in multiple embryos being implanted within a woman's uterus to maximize the chances that at least one will find a site of implantation, it's possible that more than one will be implanted, resulting in multiple births. I've mentioned multiple births previously, but it should be noted that multiples can entail far more expense years later and impact a couple's lives in terms of the time they can spend with their children or on their careers. It's an important consideration when considering IVF. It doesn't happen all the time, mind you, but the very nature of the procedure increases the possibility that it *might* happen. Nevertheless, it can be a very effective way to conceive and is one more option that may be pursued.

Perhaps the biggest drawback to the procedure is that it is enormously expensive. Most health insurance plans do not cover in vitro fertilization, which means that women interested in the procedure are responsible for its cost. Some fertility centers charge according to "cycle plans." At the Advanced Fertility Center in Chicago, for example, three plans are available (How Much Does IVF Cost at Chicago, IL, 2017). To receive IVF for a single cycle, meaning one menstrual cycle, the cost is $8,500. The second plan covers multiple cycles with no money-back guarantee. It costs $16,500. The third plan covers multiple cycles but offers a money-back guarantee if fertilization doesn't occur. It costs $18,000.

In general, the cost of IVF depends on numerous factors, and many websites offer an online calculator to take into account the following variables:

the cost of the original doctor's visit, including fertility and pre-pregnancy screening; how many ovulation cycles will be used to try for the successful implantation of an embryo; how many eggs will be harvested from the woman; how many fertility drugs will be administered before the procedure to induce the ovulation of multiple eggs; the possibility of freezing embryos (and if they are, for how long); transfer of the eggs to the uterus; blood work, including a measurement of FHS and THS levels (uterine and thyroid hormones); the age of the woman; anesthesia; and a sonohysterogram. A sonohysterogram is a procedure by which the uterus is filled with water by the insertion of a thin tube, followed by an ultrasound to gauge the shape and overall condition of the uterus (Sonohysterography, n.d.). A base cycle (IVF for a single menstrual cycle) is naturally less expensive than multiple cycles and, as seen above, one may pay extra in order to receive partial reimbursement in case fertilization doesn't occur.

The cost of an IVF at various fertility centers, therefore, varies widely from $8,000 to as much as $80,000. The more cycles that are used and the older the woman, the more the cost escalates. When considering this procedure, it's important to look at the breakdown of the various costs and to ask specialists at fertility centers about their rate of live births based on the age of the woman and number of cycles used to achieve those births.

This may sound complicated (the actual procedure as described by textbooks and medical literature would be far more complex), but it's important to know what the procedure entails since it's an option for many women dealing with infertility. Many think that IVF is just for celebrities, but nothing could be further from the truth. Even with a high price tag, the procedure is used by many women successfully to have children who are normal and healthy. I was determined as ever, plus I'd researched the procedure and wanted to know even more. Based on my research, the cost for IVF was $20,000 and I learned that scholarships were available for women who qualified. Since the procedure isn't guaranteed to work, I wanted to obtain a scholarship if at all possible.

I Googled "IVF and scholarships" and found the Baby Quest Foundation. It's an organization that provides financial assistance for women desiring high-cost procedures such as the donations of eggs and sperm, artificial insemination, egg freezing, in vitro fertilization, embryo donation, and gestational surrogacy (IVF Grants, 2014). The foundation is run by Pamela Hirsch, whose own daughter had fertility issues. On her site (babyquestfoundation.org), she relates how she helped her daughter successfully have a child by giving her financial assistance—and then wondered about the many others who also needed expensive procedures but couldn't afford them. As she says, that's when Baby Quest was born, together with co-founder Nicole Lawson.

The more I read on the website, the more I was convinced that this might be the right way to fund IVF. Indeed, maybe it was the answer to my prayers, and God himself had led me to the site. The foundation offered many great services, and it seemed to be a compassionate and knowledgeable organization that knew what women like myself had to go through to try to have a baby. It provided grants for applicants living anywhere in the United States. Applicants were under no obligation to engage in fundraising. Scholarships were given so that fertility treatments could start immediately and all staff members of the foundation had personally dealt with fertility issues, making them the ideal people to speak with since they had genuine empathy for applicants.

The application itself includes many parts, but are all straightforward. Baby Quest naturally wants salary information and employment history for the applicant and her spouse since they exist to give grants. Additionally, they request a two-page personal story related to the applicant's fertility struggles, with permission to use a synopsis of the story on their website and in promotional materials to help inform others looking into grants. Baby Quest also asks for personal photos to be used on Facebook, copies of insurance cards, a fifty dollar nonrefundable fee, and a completed medical packet. The doctor must fill out most of the latter.

But there was a problem since the medical information had to be completed by the physician who would actually perform the IVF, and Dr. Hastings didn't handle in vitro fertilization. I called the Baby Quest Foundation and, to my surprise, I didn't have to speak to a secretary or staff member. I was able to talk with Pamela Hirsch herself. I'd seen the name of a fertility specialist on the board of directors of the Baby Quest Foundation, and he not only performed IVF but practiced in the Atlanta area. I wanted to know if it would be okay if I used this physician, Dr. Peters, since I thought it might represent a conflict of interest because he was on the board at the time. Pamela enthusiastically told me that I was free to use Dr. Peters if I wished and that he was an exceptional doctor. I was overjoyed and wondered if Dr. Peters being in my geographical region was coincidence or yet another answer to prayer. My own feeling was that it was no coincidence.

I discovered the Baby Quest Foundation in August 2014 and planned on seeing Dr. Peters very soon thereafter. Meanwhile, I was engaging in colon cleansing as a natural way to enhance fertility. (This was something I did anyway, but I discovered it also had fertility applications.) Many nutrition and holistic authorities believe that the time before conception is the ideal time to cleanse the colon and detoxify the entire body, especially the liver. The liver metabolizes everything we eat and drink and it's where many toxins can accumulate. A fertility cleanse, as it is sometimes known, is a natural way to cleanse both the uterus and liver. Such cleansing stimulates the uterus to rid itself of old blood or clots and, in general, stimulates blood flow to the pelvic area. It can also help the body free itself of harmful cigarette smoke (even second-hand smoke), alcohol, prescription drugs, excessive hormones, and many harmful chemicals, such as household cleaners and pesticides, that find their way into the food chain (Rodriguez, 2017). There are many kinds of colon cleansing products on the market, and most come in the form of herbal extracts, teas, capsules, or liquids.

As noted earlier in this book, one needs to exercise caution when using any holistic approach. When taking herbs, some may be quite harmful even if recommended by an herbalist since everyone's body is different and many people have medical conditions that can be worsened by the administration of herbs (or are taking medications that adversely interact with certain herbs). A doctor should be consulted before taking any herbal product for the purposes of fertility or colon cleansing.

It is generally recommended that individuals not take any new or additional herbs while undergoing a fertility cleanse other than multivitamins or omega 3 fatty acids. Cleansing should be done before a couple actively tries to get pregnant since the regimen is designed to prepare the body before conception takes place. Also, a woman should avoid cleansing during pregnancy or if she believes she is pregnant since various herbs might be harmful to the fetus. The same applies to women who are breastfeeding since herbs can be ingested by a baby through its mother's milk. An advantage to colon cleansing is that some women find that it helps them re-establish regular periods. Finally, colon cleansing should not be regarded as a fertility treatment but only as a preparation for conception, although some women have reported getting pregnant after fertility cleansing (Rodriguez, 2017).

I remained optimistic throughout this period. I'd made payments to travel to London, Paris, and Barcelona with the Foreign Language Club on Spring Break in 2015. I was hopeful that I might be pregnant by the time of the trip and wouldn't be able to travel. I had so much faith that my personal miracle would happen that I called the travel agency to inquire about cancellation insurance since, as I told the agent, I was planning on becoming pregnant. I took out the insurance, convinced that pregnancy was getting very close, whether by natural means or in vitro fertilization.

This was at the beginning of September 2014. I would see Dr. Peters on September 11, but another big adventure awaited me the weekend before the office visit.

Summary and Points to Remember

When trying to conceive naturally failed, I was willing to try in vitro fertilization. I learned that the procedure had yielded positive results for thousands of women. It carries risks such as multiple births, and the procedure itself involves numerous steps, many of which are highly technical, time-consuming, and expensive. Hopefully, I've given you the basic information so that you can decide if this option is right for you.

I also learned that the procedure was beyond the financial means of most people but found that scholarships were available for women who were having fertility problems. In my online research, I came upon the Baby Quest Foundation. It was one of many such organizations to aid women struggling to have a baby, but the staff was friendly and I made an immediate connection with the founder.

Here are some things you should remember about in vitro fertilization and how to obtain grant money for what can potentially be an expensive procedure.

- Trying to conceive naturally doesn't mean that you exclude medicine in your quest to get pregnant. I tried both, and I wasn't hesitant to switch back and forth depending on the results I received. Look at both options and be proactive in your decision making.
- If you feel that natural methods aren't working, don't hesitate to return to your physician or OB/GYN and tell him/her what you've been trying and where you are in your quest to have a child.
- In vitro fertilization, or IVF, is a widely used procedure used to get pregnant through harvesting eggs from a woman's fallopian tubes or ovaries and having them fertilized outside the body by her husband's

sperm (or a donor's) in a dish after the sperm has been through a technical process called "sperm washing."

- There are many steps involved in IVF, and it's important to research its techniques both online and in consultation with a fertility specialist. Familiarize yourself with the steps (such as those discussed in this chapter) to help decide if IVF is right for you.

- IVF can be a highly successful method to get pregnant. Over 200,000 healthy babies have been born using the procedure, and more are being added to that number daily.

- Certain risks are attached to IVF, such as the chance of multiple births or birth defects, and these should be thoroughly discussed with your doctor before choosing this method of fertility treatment.

- IVF can be very expensive, with prices ranging from $8,000 to $80,000 or more.

- For people unable to afford the high price of IVF, grants are available through various foundations. I chose the Baby Quest Foundation.

CHAPTER SEVEN

The Life You Want Tour

Oprah Winfrey's "The Life You Want Tour" was coming to Atlanta on the weekend of September 5-6, 2014, and I needed some additional motivation before seeing Dr. Peters since other fertility methods weren't working. Oprah was touring many cities across America and her goal was to accomplish what she'd been doing on her TV show for so many years: helping people learn about themselves so they can achieve more in their lives. Oprah herself came from humble beginnings. She was born in Mississippi to a single teenage mother, but later lived in the inner city of Milwaukee, Wisconsin. From poverty to her present media empire, Oprah has known both hardship and success and is the quintessential example of someone who achieved the life she wanted. In her "Life You Want Tour," she shared her philosophy of how people can attain success in their own lives. During her talk show, which ran from 1986 to 2011, Oprah talked about spirituality and embraced Rhonda Byrnes' bestselling book, *The Secret,* on two of her shows. Oprah highlighted the book's philosophy which is based on the Law of Attraction which means that positive thinking is a powerful tool for manifesting what we want or need. Essentially, the philosophy of the book and Oprah's tour was rooted in the concept that we create our own reality by our thoughts. Negative thinking produces negative results while positive thinking creates positive results. This is a simplification of the idea, but more on that in a moment.

Oprah's tour, therefore, was not just a public appearance to chat with her audience, but rather a two-day event aimed at helping people adopt a healthier mindset, target what they want out of life, and take the basic steps to achieve it, whatever the goal might be. She toured with people such as Elizabeth Gilbert (author of *Eat, Pray, Love*), Iyanla Vanzant (inspirational speaker and life coach), Rob Bell (pastor and motivational speaker), and Deepak Chopra (doctor, author, speaker, and advocate of alternative medicine). Also, actress Amy Purdy presented an award to the founders of Black Girls Run, and her words were very inspiring. In short, the presentations during the tour were meant to empower people to reach for their dreams by shedding negativity.

All of the speakers, as well as Oprah herself, sought to impart a few basic spiritual and psychological truths to the audience. Below are my interpretations of what was presented. Crucial to success is that people embrace their current circumstances regardless of where they are in their lives and accept responsibility for them. People may not always be in possession of their dreams, but they usually have more to be thankful for than they think. Adopting a posture of gratitude is an important first step on the road to reaching a better life.

Another key point I took from the tour was that we're co-creators of our lives which means that we should be proactive rather than passive when pursuing our goals. We all have our own stories that we create—our lives are part of the decisions we've made—and we should become the heroes of our own personal narratives by taking responsibility for our choices and altering our behavior when necessary.

A third point was that we should be passionate about our calling. We all have unique talents and gifts and we're meant to share them with the world. When our lives have purpose and meaning, we're more likely to share our gifts with others. Sooner or later, they'll come back to us. As the old saying goes, we reap what we sow.

Finally, the importance of thoughts was emphasized in many of the presentations, especially by Deepak Chopra, who has long advocated that we become what we believe. Metaphysics over the ages has stated that every single thought we have in our minds emits energy, thus reinforcing what we think, believe, and do, whether it's good or bad, positive or negative. This is sometimes called mindful thinking and goes hand-in-hand with the previous points. When we're mindful, we can see more clearly where we are, what we want to become, and what we are doing—or not doing, as the case may be—to find fulfillment. We can't be the co-creators of our lives unless we are investing the energy of our thoughts in the desired outcome for our lives.

As I listened to Oprah and her speakers, these ideas resonated with me at a deep level. Indeed, I'd been a very proactive person throughout my entire life in that I had always pursued my goals with passion and energy, whether it had been to get a higher education, work in broadcasting, find a mate, or have a baby. I guess you could say that I'd already been co-creating my life for years. When it came to having a child, I had certainly taken the proverbial bull by the horns and worked holistically and with traditional medicine to try to achieve my goal. All of the ideas presented during that weekend absolutely tallied with my personal faith, which was rooted in making mountains move by believing that anything could happen. I had what the Bible calls mustard seed faith and knew that God was all-powerful, and I'd set no limits on what he could do. If I were infertile, I had certainly taken responsibility for that status by actively trying to reverse it. But that didn't mean I didn't have some work of a personal nature to do—that I didn't have room for improvement.

The tour event was broken into different parts. We were asked to picture the faces of someone we loved and then think about what we wished for them. I saw Elroy as a successful man who was financially secure and the father of a healthy boy or girl, someone happy with his life and the decisions he'd made. We were then instructed to flip that scenario and apply it to ourselves. Now I was the parent of a healthy child, someone who was happy and secure. What we wanted for our loved ones was also what we wanted for ourselves.

We were given workbooks, and one section dealt with where we were in our lives at that time. We were instructed to circle the areas that were most important regarding the lives we were striving for. The areas I circled were spirituality, faith, beliefs, family, children, and contributions to the world.

As described above, we were supposed to take responsibility for our lives and decisions and also be co-creators of our lives. We were then told to delete language that was negative and self-defeating and circle phrases that we should be using more often. In other words, if we changed our language, we would change the narrative of our lives. I crossed out phrases such as "I feel tired" or "I feel overweight" or "I feel hopeless sometimes." In their place, I circled phrases such as "I choose happiness," "I'm thankful," "I love myself," "I'm beautiful," "I am powerful," and "I can do anything."

The speaker who helped me the most was Deepak Chopra. He guided the audience through breathing exercises and meditations. As we inhaled and exhaled, I engaged in visualizations, seeing myself as happy, powerful, and the parent of a child. My vision was centered on Elroy and me being successful parents of a healthy baby boy or girl. We could attain anything, and we were grateful for the gifts God was giving to us.

Of course, meeting Oprah during the separate VIP experience was amazing all by itself. I didn't have a lengthy one-on-one sit-down discussion with her, mind you, but I did have my picture taken with her, and I was in awe of the woman who had helped so many people through the years. She is truly someone who wants to help others and the world. It was a great weekend and I completed the prescribed exercises after listening with great enthusiasm to the speakers. I'd had faith that I would conceive one day soon, but the two-day event sharpened my focus, cleared my mind of negative thinking and self-talk, and took my faith to a new level.

The icing on the cake was that a Tweet I made was used for a segment (sponsored by Oil of Olay) called "What Is Your Best Beautiful Moment?" The tweet or Instagram post was supposed to be in keeping with the theme of the entire event which asked people to relate something that had required them to reach deep down into their inner selves in order to achieve a goal that required strength and determination. I tweeted about the day I became Dr. Samantha Rogers, a graduate with a doctorate in education, and this was shared on the video screen with the entire audience. I was proud to see my personal achievement highlighted in large letters for so many people to see.

Oprah had always been a celebrity I looked up to. As I've stated, I'd watched her show since I was a teen. Having been to her workshop and then actually meeting her was an awesome experience, and during that weekend I received the energy and wisdom that so many have felt through her broadcasts. I was more convinced than ever that I could and would have a baby. I was on the right path, and the road was even straighter as a result of the advice and guidance I'd received that weekend. It was a life-changing experience.

Summary and Points to Remember

I'd been working on getting pregnant using both natural approaches and medical procedures. In my future was a discussion with a top fertility specialist, someone on the board of a prestigious foundation. But I was also still rooted in faith, and my weekend at "The Life You Want Tour" helped sharpen my vision and double my resolve to press forward in my quest to have a baby.

Not everyone can meet Oprah or even attend such an inspirational event such as her tour, but everyone *does* have opportunities to be renewed and get their energies recharged. Here are some things to consider if you need to have your own ideas refocused or simply find a new vision and get away from negative thoughts.

- Attend motivational lectures in your area if they are available and don't go against anything in your personal belief system. The speakers may not be celebrities, but such events can be very energizing and help you to rededicate yourself to having a baby.
- Through many diverse activities, you may find new purpose and passion in your quest to find the right mate, profession, or get pregnant. You may find your spirits lifted by simply attending a church social or picnic. The nature of the activity is secondary to what benefits you take away from it. Even going to see an inspirational play or movie has the potential to lift your spirits.
- Go to bookstores in your areas and find books by celebrity motivational speakers you admire. If you can't meet them personally, you can derive great hope and comfort from reading their books. You only have to get in your car and do a little browsing at a bookstore for an hour or two to come away with new ideas that can take you to the next level of fulfillment.
- Be positive in approaching your goal, and if you're reading this book, there's a good chance that your goal is to get pregnant.
- Eliminate negative self-talk and replace it with positive words, ideas, and images. You will become what you think you are.
- Consider going to activities that can enhance your ability to concentrate. There are many classes in most communities on yoga, breathing, and visualization. Such classes can be healthy for both the body and the mind.
- Be active in your church if you belong to one. Many of the ideas I heard during the Oprah tour were already integral parts of the faith I practiced.

CHAPTER EIGHT

Implementing my Vision

Meeting Oprah had been an awesome experience, and now it was time to implement the positive ideas I'd taken away from Oprah, Deepak Chopra, and the other speakers on the tour. It was one thing to write down ideas in a workbook while feeling motivated and exhilarated during the actual weekend event, but it was now back to daily life and time to really believe that I could do anything at all. It was time to replace any residual negative talk in my mind with positive thoughts and visualizations. I was ready to do just that. I had already been positive, but you might say that Oprah's speakers had put my enthusiasm on steroids.

But there are always naysayers, right? It's worth noting that people continued to offer advice that, although it was well-meaning, was more like nails on a chalkboard whenever I heard it. There was the ever-present mantra of "just relax." This was hard to listen to since I had been trying so many different methods in order to become pregnant. While I was confident that I would conceive, I was being proactive, and "just relaxing" was literally not something I had the luxury of doing.

Other people would say philosophically that "It will happen when it's supposed to happen." This is a cliché that didn't really offer me any comfort since my biological clock was ticking. I didn't for a minute think that it was "supposed to happen" when I was in my fifties or sixties. In my heart, I thought that it was supposed to happen sooner, not later. This saying is a lot like "just relax." It implies that nothing needs to be done by a woman who is trying to conceive, and as this book illustrates, one needs to consider a lot of methods, many of which entail several steps.

Some people like to ask, "Have you considered adoption?" I guess this question is to be expected, but I wanted to have my *own* children.

Realistically, adoption is the only option for many, but I firmly believed at the time (and still do) that giving up prematurely is a mistake that too many women make. It takes perseverance, and I was "in it to win it," as the saying goes.

Other people had advice of a more personal nature, such as "go on vacation, get drunk, eat more fiber, or have intercourse only in the afternoons," claiming that such activities worked for them or their friends. While I was open to any kind of solid advice, Elroy and I already traveled a lot and we knew what we were doing. Besides, I'd placed my trust in God, not in getting drunk.

Fortunately, I had a shield in place to fend off the endless advice that people offered. I had faith and also a new found optimism stemming from my weekend experience with Oprah and her entourage of motivational speakers. It was *their* advice that spoke to my heart in ways that all of the above statements could not. The things I'd heard from Elizabeth Gilbert, Deepak Chopra, and others had kindled a fire within my spirit, increasing my faith and expectation that good things were going to happen in my life, the best one being that I was going to have a baby of my own—and soon. The kinds of advice listed above, while meant as encouragement, were not that different from the negative, self-defeating inner talk that women fall prey to when trying to get pregnant, and it was that negative talk that I'd crossed out of my workbook and thinking. I was aiming for success, not idle consolation.

I, therefore, saw Dr. Peters on September 11, 2014 at a reproductive center in Atlanta and discussed my case with him, explaining all that I'd done thus far and that my goal was still to have a baby. I told him how I'd found his name and that I was interested in having in vitro fertilization. I felt very much at home in this atmosphere since the reproductive center offers friendly surroundings and individualized treatment for infertility based on a woman's medical history and background in attempting to become pregnant. The center has a world-class staff trained in infertility issues and embryology. I was definitely in the right place, and it had turned out to be in my own backyard, so to speak. Was this another sign from God that he was walking side-by-side with me? I hoped so.

But there was a problem. By Body Mass Index, known as BMI, was too high, and this precluded my ability to move forward with IVF. Body Mass Index measures the amount of tissue mass in an individual, including muscle, fat, and bone, in order to characterize an individual as underweight, normal, or overweight. The actual mathematical formula for gauging someone's BMI uses a person's weight, height, and body contours.

If a woman's BMI is too high, then IVF can be problematic for several reasons. If a woman is overweight, her ovaries are usually pushed higher in her body and farther away from her vagina, making egg retrieval (described previously) harder and less safe. Also, increased fatty tissue makes ultrasound images fuzzier, and makes it more difficult for a doctor to see the needle he or she is inserting into the ovarian follicles to harvest the eggs for future fertilization outside the body. This means that sometimes fewer eggs are retrieved and increased bleeding can occur during the procedure if the patient is overweight (Weight BMI and Fertility and IVF Success, 2017).

Other complications can also arise during or after IVF if a woman's Body Mass Index is too high. Higher body mass can result in a greater chance of miscarriage, and that was not something I took lightly for obvious reasons. Furthermore, a high BMI increases the risk of still birth, pre-eclampsia, gestational diabetes, and hypertension. There are also greater risks when overweight women deliver vaginally, and many need caesarean sections. For the reasons cited, fertility doctors will often recommend many different methods to lower the BMI number, such as diets, nutritional counseling, and exercise programs (The Effect of Weight on Fertility, 2016). A high BMI can affect women of any age who are pregnant or want to become pregnant, and this applies all the more to women who are older and are already at risk for certain complications. I understood this completely since the procedure carries various risks in and of itself, and it would be irresponsible for any physician not to reduce as much risk as possible before IVF is undertaken. Fertility treatment is all about increasing a woman's chance of getting pregnant, and that, in turn, involves minimizing those factors that might result in a negative outcome.

Dr. Peters, however, was very understanding and said that if I could lower my BMI, then I would be a candidate for the procedure. Also, he told me that since I was determined to lose the weight, he would schedule me for Family Prep Screening. This screening would analyze my DNA to look for rare or dangerous genetic diseases that might be passed to a child. The test would be done by Counsyl, a Silicon Valley start-up company that markets itself as able to prevent more than one hundred diseases through genetic screening before pregnancy, including such diseases as cystic fibrosis, Tay-Sachs, sickle cell disease, and many others. The company claims that many of the diseases it screens for are either fatal or incurable. The test analyzes a person's DNA by collecting saliva from a patient and the actual analysis of the DNA is expensive (Pollack, 2010).

I underwent the screening in September 2014 and my results came back negative which meant that no abnormalities had been detected. This was good news so in the meantime, I decided to embark upon an exercise regimen in order to lower my BMI. I began working out with a personal trainer, Neil, owner of Mindworx Fitness. Neil was good and really put me through the paces two days each week. I did jumping jacks, knee crunches, jump squats, a lot of walking on the treadmill and many other exercises. It was hard work (not a question of "just relax" at all!) and I threw myself into it since I wanted to undergo IVF. I'd made a connection with Baby Quest and Dr. Peters, and I felt that I was in good hands and was pointed in the right direction. Strenuous exercise was not something that would deter me from reaching my goal. As far as I was concerned, I'd found a fertility treatment that could give me a baby, so I worked with Neil and religiously did the homework he gave me. In addition to working out, I completed a two-day fasting cleansing detox and changed my diet reducing sugar intake and eating smaller portions. It was also good for my overall health, and anything that increases the general health of a woman can increase her chances of becoming pregnant at any age. I was increasing my odds of having a child and taking care of my own body at the same time. In short, I was implementing my vision by enlisting the most advanced fertility treatment that medicine had to offer, and I was willing to work out if that was a prerequisite for IVF.

As always, life went on as usual. Elroy and I attended our church picnic in September, and I chaperoned a trip to the Georgia State Fair, sharing with two of my colleagues from school my desire to have a baby. One of them had also struggled with fertility but went on to have a healthy baby boy. In October, I was on fall break and Elroy and I went to Miami to celebrate our third wedding anniversary.

When I got married, I originally thought that I'd have had a baby by this time or at least be pregnant. It hadn't happened, but I wasn't depressed or resigned. Forty is just a number and I hadn't lost hope. Too many women in my age bracket were having healthy children, and although my BMI was high, I was otherwise healthy and no test had ever shown that my reproductive system was incapable of conceiving and bearing a child. I was still harboring the positive vibes from Oprah's tour and keeping firm my trust in God, who can do all things. I was going to move ahead and expect the best.

Summary and Points to Remember

After attending "The Life You Want Tour" in Atlanta, I felt very focused and optimistic. I shook off the comments of many people who tried to offer advice or said, "Are you *still* thinking about having a baby?" In fact, I was more determined than ever. I kept my appointment with Dr. Peters who, though encouraging in his overall assessment of my situation, informed me that I had to lower my Body Mass Index, or BMI, since being overweight can cause complications for older women who want to undergo in vitro fertilization.

Noting my willingness to work out and get in shape in order to drop my BMI number, Dr. Peters had me genetically screened by a relatively new company called Counsyl that looked for possible genetic abnormalities in women who wished to conceive. I tested negative and began working out while carrying on with my work at school and my life with Elroy. I remained confident and kept my self-talk positive, always visualizing success.

Here are the points I want you to remember based on my experiences described in this chapter.

- Don't let well-intentioned advice get you down if you're not having success in conceiving. In fact, you should probably expect people who are aware of your efforts to get pregnant to offer numerous bits of advice and clichés described at the beginning of this chapter. When you encounter such advice, don't let it deter you or cause you to deviate from a path of faith, hope, and proactive steps. Keep your thoughts positive and don't be dissuaded from your goal. Remember that you, not others, are in charge of your destiny.
- If you wish to investigate in vitro fertilization as a fertility treatment, seek a doctor who is a fertility specialist. There are many fertility clinics around the country that offer state-of-the-art procedures such as intrauterine insemination, in vitro fertilization, and other services for women with any number of fertility issues.
- Your Body Mass Index, or BMI, is important when considering IVF. If your BMI number is too high, it means you're overweight. Excessive tissue in your reproductive area can make it difficult for a physician to insert the needle into your ovaries and see its placement on an ultrasound. Also, the number of eggs that can be harvested may be fewer in number. Finally,

a high BMI is associated with various medical complications during pregnancy.

- If your BMI is too high, don't despair. Consider altering your diet and starting an exercise regimen in order to lose weight. If you fall into this category, find a fertility specialist who is willing to work with you rather than giving you a flat refusal in regards to performing the procedure.

- Research the physicians and fertility treatment centers in your area and gather as much information on them as possible before you make a selection or schedule an appointment. It's important to have confidence in the doctor and clinic you select. Ask about the center's success rate and staff. If necessary, set up an initial consultation without necessarily committing to using the treatment center's services. This is one of the most important decisions of your life, so screen fertility centers closely and choose one that can address your particular needs based on your medical history and any prior fertility treatments you may have received.

- Most fertility centers will ask you to undergo DNA screening to assess the risk of passing on genetic diseases. A positive result does not necessarily mean that you will produce offspring that will have a given disease, but the screening is usually part of a center's overall fertility counseling.

CHAPTER NINE

BFP

I lost twelve pounds as a result of working out, detoxing and changing my diet. I was well on my way to reaching that all-important goal of shedding thirty pounds so that Dr. Peters could perform in vitro fertilization. I'd accomplished this in about six weeks, which wasn't really that much time. If I continued on course and stuck with my exercise routine, I thought I could reach my goal in a few more months, and I was more confident than ever. I'd received acupuncture and reflexology, I'd used the OvaCue monitor, had rededicated myself to prayer and reciting Bible verses, and had been inspired by Oprah and her team of motivational speakers. I was as enthusiastic as anyone could be.

After a faculty meeting one day, a teacher Adrianne, and I were talking about life in general and to my surprise, she asked "What are you waiting on to have children?" (not everyone was aware of my struggles to get pregnant). So many were encouraging in the best way possible, as opposed to those who would say, "Just relax. It will happen when it's supposed to happen." I'd heard this question before and thought I was about to hear more of the same idle pep talk. I explained to her that getting pregnant wasn't as easy as it sounded.

"You need to take some Geritol!" she exclaimed.

I was skeptical of this advice and wondered if it were any different than "Get drunk since that is what my husband and I did." It sounded a bit simplistic, and I needed proof. My research had shown that certain practices increased fertility, such as colon cleansing or massages, but just taking Geritol sounded too easy. I asked her if she actually knew anyone who'd taken the popular supplement and gotten pregnant, and she said that she did. In fact, she claimed it had worked for a couple of people fairly quickly. I ran out to Walgreen's, purchased Geritol pills, and went home and looked up "Geritol and pregnancy" on my computer. Sure enough, I found dozens of websites and blogs related to getting pregnant after taking Geritol. I also saw on many of these sites the statement that "There's a baby in every bottle." That certainly got my attention. Preliminary research showed that Geritol was a multivitamin especially rich in iron. In fact, Geritol had been advertised on television many years ago as a remedy for "iron-poor blood," or a form of anemia in which the blood does not have enough hemoglobin. Hemoglobin is a protein in red blood cells that helps transport oxygen throughout the body.

I decided to go straight to the source and clicked on the Geritol website and saw that it was indeed a multivitamin supplement rich in iron, B vitamins, and pantothenic acid. The website had a disclaimer that read, "There is, unfortunately, no evidence that specifically taking Geritol can increase fertility or your chances of getting pregnant. We don't make any fertility claims and we're not quite sure how the rumor got started" (Will Geritol Multivitamin Increase My Fertility?, 2014).

I found a blog, however, that advocated Geritol as a surefire way to get pregnant. It was by PinkPadUser, who said that she was eight weeks pregnant with her fourth child. Admitting that she was no expert, she nevertheless said that taking Geritol and following certain protocols had worked for her and her friends. Her advice was very precise. She wrote that a woman trying to get pregnant should buy a bottle of Geritol tonic, take the liquid for a week prior to ovulation and during the entire week that she's fertile. Furthermore, she said that husbands should take the tonic as well. Finally, she advocated that women should exercise thirty minutes a day to stimulate blood flow, drink plenty of water, and use an ovulation calculator (PinkPadUser, 2012). I went to the drug store again, bought the tonic, and began to take it, not the pills. I was already taking folic acid and a prenatal vitamin, but besides the Geritol, I added biotin and resumed using the OvaCue monitor. There was no harm in trying it since Geritol was an over-the-counter product that had been used for years and was a multivitamin supplement enhanced with a healthy dose of iron. My co-worker seemed to think it would be helpful, and countless testimonies online, such as the one by PinkPadUser, seemed to think that it was virtually a magic elixir. I had faith in medicine and, as already noted, was skeptical of people's homespun remedies for infertility, but the vast number of blogs, websites, and forums that mentioned Geritol went beyond folksy advice or clichés. Something good seemed to be happening to women taking this vitamin and iron supplement, and so I thought that it was worth a try. Using common sense, I'd tried numerous methods as cited in earlier chapters, and one more weapon in my arsenal to combat infertility couldn't hurt.

I was still exercising with an eye to lowering my BMI and having IVF, so I was keeping in shape and increasing the circulation throughout my body. All exercise, cardio and otherwise, is beneficial to the body because it oxygenates cells, tissues, and organs. Oxygen is what cells need to carry out their various functions in the body. Additionally, when our cells are functioning properly, they're not only doing what they were designed to do genetically, but they release toxins into the bloodstream so that they can be eliminated from the body. As stated above, iron-rich blood helps the body maintain a healthy supply of red blood cells—cells that transport oxygen throughout the circulatory system. In fact, massage, yoga, deep breathing, and stretching are all associated with an increased blood flow of oxygen to the cells of our bodies. When our bodies are oxygenated, the heart pumps more efficiently, brain cells function more clearly, the liver detoxifies the body more thoroughly, and, in the case of women, the uterus and fallopian tubes are more capable of carrying out their roles in ovulation, conception, and implantation. The makers of Geritol may have added a disclaimer to their website after years of advertising that "There's a baby in every bottle," but the theory of giving the body more vitamins, minerals, and oxygen seemed sound.

During the fall of 2014, I continued to "pray without ceasing" since, for me, God was my ultimate source of strength, and if I got pregnant it was going to be as a result of putting my trust in him. As far as I was concerned, he could use whatever method he wanted, whether it was IVF or a tonic rich in iron and vitamins. In considering God's promise in the Old Testament to Abraham and Sarah that they would conceive a child in their advanced years, it's important to understand that he didn't tell them *how* he was going to do it, only that he would. I firmly believe in the saying that "God works in mysterious ways his wonders to perform." This is not actually a verse from scripture, although it is implied in many books of the Bible.

I traveled to Birmingham on October 25 for the Magic City Classic— Alabama State University (my alumni school) versus Alabama A&M. I felt good, and my daily routine of going to work was unvaried. I was anticipating going to Dr. Peters one day soon, proudly announcing that I'd lost thirty pounds and that we could start filling out the paperwork to get my scholarship with The Baby Quest Foundation. Of course, if I turned up pregnant, that would be fine, too.

On November 3, I was too tired to go through my workout routine and went home and got straight into bed. I assumed that my body was being affected by Daylight Savings Time since I'd lost an hour of sleep when the clocks changed and the amount of sunlight had decreased. (A sudden decrease in exposure to sunlight can alter people's circadian rhythms, causing them to take several days to adjust to the time change.) But two weeks later I missed my period. Although I had experienced irregular periods in the past, I suspected that I might be pregnant because I felt an unusual stretching sensation in the bottom of my abdomen. I wasn't sure, however, so I told no one, not even Elroy. I needed confirmation before I shared the news with anyone. I didn't want to urinate on a stick that came with a home pregnancy test, so I went to an Any Lab Test Now center to get a blood test—and I hate needles almost as much as peeing on a stick. The results, I was told, would be emailed to me the next day. I went home and waited anxiously. It had been over three years since Elroy and I had gotten married and started trying to have a baby. I prayed and hoped, which was all I could really do. The matter was in God's hands.

When I opened the email the following day, I was confused because it said that the test was positive/abnormal. Positive? Abnormal? Was I pregnant or not? I called Any Lab Test Now, hoping they could explain the results. I was connected to a technician and told her what the email said, and asked if she could clarify what "positive/abnormal" meant in this context. She said that she wasn't allowed to give out that kind of information. I respected her position and politely told her that although I understood the company's policy, I had to know one way or the other. She hesitated and paused briefly while hanging on the telephone line before cautiously saying that she couldn't *confirm* that the result meant I was pregnant. Confirm? I interpreted her brief moment of silence and careful wording to mean that I was indeed pregnant. She had tried to validate my belief "in between the lines," as far as I was concerned.

And yet the tech still hadn't come out and told me the exact words I'd wanted to hear for the past three years. I called Dr. Hastings' office and told them about the results—that I *thought* I was pregnant—and the nurse asked me what my HCG level was. I had no idea, so I went back to Any Lab Test Now the very next day for another test in order to measure my HCG, which, as mentioned earlier, stands for Human Chorionic Gonadotropin, a hormone produced by the placenta after the implantation of an embryo. I had to know for myself since my next appointment with Dr. Hastings was still a few days away. The HCG levels were increased and right where they should be at five weeks of gestation. Based on my last missed period, five weeks earlier was exactly when I estimated that I would have conceived. I was pregnant!

I went to Dr. Hastings' office on November 24 and brought my results from Any Lab Test Now. Dr. Hastings did an ultrasound and was able to see the yolk sac very clearly. It resembled a tiny bubble that, when magnified, looked like the tip of my pinky finger. I was elated and began to laugh.

"Why are you laughing at your baby?" Dr. Hastings asked.

The answer was quite simple. I now had a BFP, a "big fat positive," and what I'd dreamed of for so long was finally happening. I was going to have a baby! If I'd known that Dr. Hastings was going to be able to see the sac so clearly, I would have brought Elroy with me so he could have shared in the very first viewing of our child. Nevertheless, I was overcome with joy. In vitro fertilization wouldn't be necessary. I had tried many different things, both mainstream and alternative, and now my persistence had paid off. God had heard my prayer and was granting my dearest wish. A mountain had moved in my life, and what I'd asked for and visualized was coming to pass.

I was also laughing because when I miscarried, the doctor at the hospital who performed my ultrasound had told me that she couldn't see the yolk sac. No baby was visible on the imaging, causing her to say that I'd probably miscarried. Dr. Hastings, however, was able to see the sac clearly, and the contrast between the two events was so profound that I couldn't contain myself.

I naturally gave thanks to God and attributed the happy outcome to him, but what specifically in the earthly realm had triggered ovulation and conception? I still don't have a definitive answer to that question to this day. In retrospect, however, I believe that losing twelve pounds as a result of working out with Neil, in conjunction with taking Geritol, was what caused me to conceive. I can't say for sure that Geritol was the magic ingredient that made everything fall into place, but by the same token I don't think it was pure coincidence. Perhaps the best way to express it is that I think Geritol was a catalyst for my pregnancy. I believe that the iron, vitamins, minerals, and oxygenation of my blood, together with my fall exercise regimen, had worked together and helped me to conceive a baby. However, I can't emphasize enough that even though I can point to these two factors as possible reasons for my BFP, I don't discount my positive attitude, my visualizations, my refusal to give up, and my prayer life. Perhaps God looked with favor on all of these actions, as well as my faith, and blessed me with such a great gift, which was that I was going to be his vehicle for bringing another life into the world. Maybe God had led me to the idea of IVF and then a visit with Dr. Peters so that I would lose those twelve pounds. Maybe weight loss was part of his plan, and even though I hadn't needed IVF, Dr. Peters' advice was probably instrumental in my becoming pregnant. Perhaps God also led me to Neil who, with the arduous regimen of exercise he'd prescribed to lose the weight, had been instrumental in helping me to achieve my goal. Then again, maybe God had prompted my co-worker to speak to me about Geritol, and then prompted me further by having me find the blog by PinkPadUser who adamantly believed in her own fertility plan, which included Geritol as a key ingredient. As St. Paul says in Romans 8:28, "And we know that in all things God works for the good of those who love him, who have been called according to his purpose." God's ways are inscrutable, and it's possible that he placed certain ideas in my mind and people in my path to achieve a single goal. I realize that there are those who will say that much of the above can be explained as good luck or in rational terms of simple cause and effect. I respect their opinions, but in my heart I know what I believe. The mountain had been moved by mustard seed faith. I'd asked and received. I'd knocked and the door had been opened for me.

I was now able to share the good news with Elroy, and he was elated, to say the least. Elroy is not the kind of person who, in any circumstance, would jump up and down or give people high fives. It's just not who he is. He's a quiet man, but that doesn't mean he doesn't have emotions. When I told him the news, he blinked, smiled, and said how glad he was that we would become parents. It was the moment we had waited for, and I thought back to the time when I'd been looking for a new tenant for my rental property, my eyes straying to the personal ads on a popular website. If I hadn't taken a chance on contacting him, and if he hadn't turned out to be such an intelligent, thoughtful, and patient man, maybe we wouldn't have been sharing this beautiful and special moment. Other men might have thought me to be impatient about having a baby and become frustrated or annoyed with all of my praying and visits to various doctors and clinics, but not Elroy. He had been the perfect man for me and had shown up at just the right time. This, too, to my way of thinking, was more than just a coincidence. God had put him in the right place at the right time.

Elroy was scheduled to go to Dr. Peters' office on November 25 for his genetic screening through the services of Counsyl, and I accompanied him so that I could thank Dr. Peters face-to-face and tell him how grateful I was that he'd urged me to lower my Body Mass Index. During this joint visit, I also told Dr. Peters about my taking Geritol, working out, and weight loss. He smiled but was inclined to believe that it was the exercise and weight loss had done the trick. Either way, he was happy for me and told Elroy there was no reason for him to undergo genetic screening since I was now pregnant.

A few days later I attended the baby shower of a friend and started to get ideas about games for my own baby shower. It was a wonderful event because I was no longer an outsider looking in. I myself was going to have a baby, and soon it would be *my* turn to have a shower. I was so happy that I was probably glowing. By the same token, Elroy and I decided not to share the news with anyone except my mother, sisters, and Kia, best friend from college. For everybody else, we were going to observe the three-month rule. I wasn't going to do anything foolish or tempt fate. I would wait the usual period of time before making a public announcement.

I was nervous at the beginning of my pregnancy due to my previous miscarriage. I was worried that I'd get up one morning and see blood or spotting when I used the bathroom. I hadn't lost faith in God, but it was a normal human reaction in light of what had transpired in February 2013. Two things, however, allayed my fears. First, I heard the baby's heartbeat during a subsequent ultrasound and discovered that once the fetal heartbeat is detected, the chances for a miscarriage are extremely rare. In fact, once the heartbeat of a fetus is detected as strong and healthy, there is only a four percent chance of miscarriage (Danielsson, 2017). This was very heartening, to say the least. The heartbeat was, quite literally, music to my ears. The steady, rhythmical drumming of my child's heart told me that it—whether he or she—was off to the best start possible.

Additionally, I'd confided with my preacher regarding my fears, and his response was an unequivocal "Let that go!" He was, of course, absolutely correct. It was negative self-talk, and I could imagine Oprah or Deepak Chopra standing before me, urging me to focus on what I wanted and not to entertain fear-based thinking. And they would have been right. I was "thinking for two now," to modify an old adage, and with my baby still part of my own body, I wanted to send all the positive messages I could to my baby. Medical doctors and psychologists, including physicians who are specialists in prenatal health and psychology, agree that a mother's emotions are transmitted to her unborn child by way of neurohormones. Stress-related hormones can cause unborn babies to feel fear and depression, and these emotions can even determine how children will develop psychologically after they're born. Conversely, Dr. Deepak Chopra has stated often that positive thoughts of happiness, security, and health will cause the pregnant woman's body to produce beneficial hormones and peptides, such as endorphins and encephalins, which will give the baby feelings of hope, optimism, and happiness. This is not speculation, but rather is based on research and tracking studies conducted by prenatal specialists (Goodlatte, 2014).

I also had the strong support of co-worker, Ms. Joycelyn Reid. She'd come to my wedding and had informed me that she was waiting for the next big step, which was for me to have a baby. Now that I was pregnant, she was encouraging and took care of me in so many ways. She was "old school," loved to cook, and brought me breakfast on many mornings and always made sure I was eating properly.

I was feeling much better after hearing my baby's heartbeat and listening to my minister. I had every reason to expect a terrific outcome, and it was my duty to make sure my baby felt the same way!

Was Dr. Samantha Rogers Fitts going to have a normal, healthy baby? She certainly was!

Summary and Points to Remember

I'd been thinking in terms of having in vitro fertilization. Surely, I thought, this was the way I would eventually conceive. I'd done the work of finding scholarship money and a doctor who would perform the procedure, one who was well known and was actually on the board of the Baby Quest Foundation. It was, to me, a marriage made in heaven, pun intended. A roadblock appeared, however, when I finally met Dr. Peters since he told me that my BMI, or Body Mass Index, was too high. He would perform the IVF, but only if I lost thirty pounds. In the meantime, I went ahead with genetic screening by Counsyl since I was committed to losing the weight.

Life continued in a normal fashion, and after finding out I was not carrying any DNA markers that would pass genetic abnormalities to a baby, I dedicated myself to strenuous workouts with my personal trainer, always remembering to keep praying since, for me, God was the bottom line.

During a normal conversation with a co-worker, I was advised to start taking Geritol and get on with the business of having a baby. To my surprise, preliminary research showed that more than a few women claimed they'd conceived after taking Geritol tonic even though the pharmaceutical company that manufactures the product had a disclaimer that they had no scientific documentation to back up such claims. Nevertheless, I took the tonic since it was simply a potent multivitamin.

Within weeks, I'd missed my period, and it was confirmed both by an independent lab test and Dr. Hastings' ultrasound that I was indeed pregnant. Although initially concerned that I might miscarry a second time, I heard the baby's heartbeat and was reassured that medical statistics indicated that a miscarriage was highly unlikely once the heartbeat is detected by an ultrasound. Not surprisingly, God had come through. I'd received a BFP, a Big Fat Positive result, and was on my way to putting that final piece in place in order to live the life I'd always envisioned for myself.

Here are the most important points from this chapter.

- If you're considering IVF, remember that certain conditions must be met. Fertility specialists will evaluate your weight, the number and quality of your eggs, offer nutritional advice, and inform you as to whether they deem you a good candidate for the procedure.
- Exercise and eating healthy is an important part in your prenatal planning if you're having trouble conceiving. Exercise is capable of lowering your weight (which in many cases makes conception easier) and also helps oxygenate your body, including your uterus. It helps tone your muscles, including your reproductive organs.
- Taking a prenatal multivitamin is important, and most OB/GYN doctors and fertility specialists will prescribe such a supplement in order to make sure your body is getting all of the vital nutrients, vitamins, and minerals it needs to conceive.
- Many women claim that Geritol, a tonic containing high concentrations of vitamins and iron (especially B Vitamins), has helped them get pregnant. While taking this supplement is very popular among women in all age brackets who wish to have a child or are having trouble conceiving, there is no medical research that validates this belief, and the manufacturers of Geritol have issued disclaimers that they do not market the pills or the

tonic as a fertility aid. If you choose to take this supplement, you may want to check with your physician depending on whether or not you are already taking a prenatal vitamin or other nutritional supplements.

- Remain steadfast in your desire to have a child even if it's taking time to conceive. Don't let casual comments or random advice discourage you or dissuade you from a course of sensible steps, medical or holistic, to realize your dream of having a child.

- If you believe you're pregnant, get confirmation from your doctor as soon as possible so that you can determine whether or not you've conceived. Don't wait until you think you *might* have conceived. The sooner you get confirmation, even if it's from an independent lab, the sooner you can schedule visits with your OB/GYN doctor to begin prenatal care.

- Once you know you're pregnant, stay positive and hopeful throughout your gestational months. Remember that your thoughts and emotions will affect your baby's development.

CHAPTER TEN

Prenatal Care

Elroy and I were planning on telling his family the good news on Christmas morning in Littleton exactly four years to the day after he'd gotten down on his knee to propose to me—the very same time and the very same place. It seemed a fitting thing to do since that's where our personal odyssey together had started, an odyssey that included three years of trying to have a baby together. We were all set to go, but his father called to say there were problems with the septic tank at their family home and that we wouldn't be able to use the restroom in the house. Instead, we would have to go across the street to his uncle's house to use the restroom. That posed a problem since pregnant women have to urinate frequently, and I was no exception. I couldn't picture myself getting up to walk across the street every time I had to relieve myself, so Elroy and I decided to spend Christmas Day in our home in Atlanta. We spent Christmas morning calling his father, brother, and other family members to share the news that we were going to have a baby.

The year 2015 started out great since this really was a "new year" for us. It would mark the beginning of a new life and a radical change in the lives of Elroy and myself, but we were ready for it. Overall, I felt great, and my morning sickness was minimal. We went to the Westin Hotel to bring in the New Year, listening to Chandra Currelley and her band. It was a special evening for us because we had so much anticipation for all of the events that 2015 would witness.

Shortly after Elroy and I were married, his brother and wife, who had a boy and a girl, asked us whether or not we intended to have children. We naturally said that we wanted a family, and they told us that they had retained a doula, informing us how helpful their own doula had been. The word "doula" is Greek and means "women's servant." A doula plays many different roles, aiding mothers who are expecting, actually delivering, or offering support for those who have already given birth. The term usually refers to a "birth doula," however, or a "labor companion," someone who is present at a birth to provide emotional and physical support to the mother.

The relationship between a doula and mother usually begins months before the baby's due date. The relationship exists so that the doula can answer questions about birth or help alleviate fears the mother may have. The doula can also inform the expectant mother about pain-relieving techniques or possible complications that can occur during the later months of pregnancy or during the delivery itself. In general, the doula helps the mother develop a birth plan, which will be discussed later (Having a Doula: Is a Doula For Me?, 2017)

One morning I was watching a television special on having children, and the program featured a doula named Teresa. I immediately connected with the topics she was covering related to childbirth, and I went online to bookmark her website in case I needed it in the future. When I told Elroy's brother that I'd seen Teresa on the TV special, he told me that this was the very doula he and his wife had used for the births of their own children. It was another connection that I thought was surely divine in nature. Elroy and I contracted with Teresa, a doula and the founder of Atlanta-based Labor of Love Doula & Childbirth Services, in January.

Labor of Love Doula & Childbirth Services included labor services, antepartum and postpartum services, childbirth classes, lactation services, placenta encapsulation, massage therapy, and soothing sessions (Our Classes, 2017). Soothing Sessions are provided by a postpartum professional, who gives a three hour course to help families as soon as the baby is brought home and includes information on breastfeeding, newborn care, sleep ideas, and child safety (New Family Soothing Sessions, 2017).

The two main classes offered by Labor of Love Doula & Childbirth Services are the Wisdom for Birth Series and The Fundamentals for an Empowered Birth classes. The Wisdom for Birth Series is divided into three classes. These include a full day in the BOLD Women's Circle, four and a half hours in the Aligned and Ready Workshop, and a full day (sometimes a weekend) for Couples Classes. The Fundamentals for an Empowered Birth is a twelve hour class for a couple expecting a baby and, through videos and discussion, facilitates the desired birth experience.

These services offered exactly what I was looking for: a natural and holistic way to have a baby, one that would include the mind-body connection in preparation for birth as well as the actual delivery. This didn't mean I wasn't going to see my OB/GYN during pregnancy, but rather that I wanted to integrate my entire birth experience with a natural approach since I'd been interested in holistic health and the mind-body connection for many years prior to becoming pregnant.

My new physician was Dr. Clemmons, who was affiliated with Alliant OB/GYN, which was an obstetrics and gynecology practice in Atlanta. I began my prenatal care with Dr. Clemmons in December and saw other doctors who practiced in the Alliant Group, although Dr. Clemmons was my major provider and was the one who performed my ultrasounds.

Despite all of the positive feedback I'd gotten early on in my pregnancy, such as being able to hear the baby's heartbeat, I was considered to be high-risk due to my weight and age. I didn't want to do anything that might trigger a miscarriage even though I'd been told that this was unlikely to happen, and I would at times become concerned between doctor's visits if I didn't feel the baby move. I began reading pregnancy blogs on a regular basis, and some of the information was positive and some of it was decidedly negative and worrisome. Some blogs, for example, cautioned women about eating certain foods or wearing various cosmetics, such as nail polish. One even advised against getting a pedicure. There are many myths and wives tales about pregnancy, and it was hard to determine fact from fiction. It was theoretically possible that certain chemicals absorbed by the human body, even through the skin, could cross the placenta and enter the baby's bloodstream, so I sometimes called the nursing line at Alliant. I was also concerned that eating queso Mexican sauce, one of my favorite foods, might be dangerous since queso has been known to contain listeria, a bacteria found in dairy products, one that often targets pregnant women, newborns, and the elderly. I became so absorbed in the warnings on these blogs that a co-worker told me to stay away from them since I was cultivating a habit of needless worry. I followed her advice and even ate queso sauce without experiencing any negative effects.

On January 7, 2015, which was twelve weeks into gestation, Dr. Clemmons performed an ultrasound and said that, based on what he saw, there was a seventy-five percent chance that my baby was a girl. Although we'd been hoping for a boy, the old saying applied: as long as it's healthy and has all of its fingers and toes! And this was exactly the case with my baby. By this time, the doctor and I could see that the baby did indeed have five fingers, plus we could see her organs developing, and everything looked normal. We could not only hear the heartbeat, but also knew the heart rate, which was exactly what it should have been at twelve weeks. While I was technically considered to be high-risk, Dr. Clemmons himself was very encouraging and upbeat and remained that way throughout my pregnancy. His prenatal care was both professional and amazing. I couldn't have asked for anyone better.

Dr. Clemmons asked Elroy and I about having a genetic screening completed for baby Fitts that was more accurate than traditional tests that predict Down syndrome and other disorders. Down syndrome is known scientifically as trisomy 21. A trisomy is a condition in which some cells contain three chromosomes rather than the usual two, with each parent donating one of the two chromosomes. Dr. Clemmons recommended that we use the Harmony Prenatal Test, which he said screened for this trisomy and others with a great deal of reliability. Harmony uses a blood sample and is reported to yield fewer false positive results than other tests. It can be done as early as ten weeks into the pregnancy and doesn't require as many office visits. Because it's done during the first trimester, it is less likely that a doctor will later recommend an invasive procedure such as amniocentesis to look for Down syndrome or genetic abnormality (Harmony Prenatal Test, 2017).

Elroy and I were in agreement and said no to the test. We both stated that the outcome of the test would make no difference since we wanted the child regardless of what the results might be. If the child were born with Down syndrome, then we would be the best parents of a child with Down syndrome. Dr. Clemmons countered that the test had the additional advantage of confirming the sex of the baby. This was naturally of interest to us since Dr. Clemmons had thus far only told us that there was a high probability that the baby was a girl. Being as inquisitive as any other couple, we reluctantly said yes. I received a call on my cell phone two weeks later while I was teaching a Thursday evening class (I worked throughout my pregnancy and continued until the end of the semester in May), and fortunately took the call since it was Dr. Clemmons's office. I wasn't apprehensive since the nurse on the other end of the line was upbeat and enthusiastic as soon as she started to speak. She said that the test results indicated that the baby was normal in every respect and showed no trace of Down syndrome. I'd concluded as much from the tone of her voice, but then she added, "Are you ready to find out the sex of your baby?" I said yes and was told that it was definitely a girl.

At home, I shared the good news with Elroy, and we immediately started researching baby names. We wanted something with a religious meaning and decided on Nadia Grace. Nadia meant "hope," and Grace meant "a gift from God." It was the perfect name given my fertility struggles and the wonderful outcome that God had given us. Nadia Grace was just that: a gift from God.

I was far enough along so that we could now make a public announcement with confidence and pride. The initial hurdles had been cleared and my pregnancy was a textbook case of normalcy. Elroy and I had a photograph taken of us holding up a sign that read:

WE PRAYED AND
HE ANSWERED!
BABY FITTS DUE
JULY 2015

During winter break, my good friend and co-worker, known as "Dr. B.," picked me up and took me to Babies "R" Us to complete the registry for presents and baby showers. It was an awesome experience to actually pick out the things that the baby I was carrying would see or use at some point in her early life. The dream was really happening, and with each passing week, doctor's visit, or medical test, the reality that I was going to have a child became more tangible. I should also add that Dr. B. advised me throughout the pregnancy and was always at my side when I had a question or concern.

It goes without saying that I continued to "pray unceasingly." My sorority sister and colleague Faustina and I often prayed together for a healthy pregnancy. God had helped me conceive, but as a person of faith I knew that getting pregnant was just the first step on a much longer journey. I realized that I would need him to help me in the days and years ahead as well.

Summary and Points to Remember

The year 2015 started out with the glorious news that I was expecting. Elroy and I decided to withhold the news from everyone except our families. We told my mother, sister, and his family in Littleton, North Carolina.

We also decided to use the services of a doula, who is essentially a trained and licensed birth companion to provide the expectant mother (or those who have already delivered) with emotional and physical support and to provide a birth plan for the mother. We chose Teresa at Labor of Love Doula & Childbirth Services in Atlanta.

I switched doctors since Dr. Hastings no longer delivered babies, choosing Dr. Clemmons with Alliant OB/GYN in Atlanta. Dr. Clemmons was very supportive despite the medical group's assessment that my pregnancy was technically high risk because of my age and weight. He performed an ultrasound that showed my baby was developing normally, and a genetic screening revealed that no genetic abnormalities such as Down syndrome were present. The screening also confirmed Dr. Clemmons's belief that we were having a girl, so we decided on the name Nadia Grace.

Here are some points to remember if you're older and have learned that you've become pregnant.

- It's natural to be anxious about your pregnancy, whether you're in your twenties (or younger) or are an older woman. It makes no difference whether you're having your first child or your fourth. You're carrying a human life within you and it's normal to have concerns. Don't let every bit of advice from the internet or your friends, family, and co-workers send you into a panic. Just as people offer advice on how to get pregnant, you'll most likely encounter many who think they know everything about giving birth based on their own experiences or those of friends. Be discriminating about who you listen to. Some people may have valuable insights, while others may be spreading myths and wives tales. If you go online, remember that you can find anything you're looking for regarding pregnancy, both good and bad. In the end, rely on your personal physician for definitive matters when worries arise.

- Don't neglect prenatal care. You need to get a complete physical workup to take care of your own health, as well as that of your baby. You should receive lab work and blood tests, ultrasounds, and physical examinations from a board certified OB/GYN. Make sure that you discuss nutrition and prenatal vitamins with your doctor. Your baby cannot develop properly if he or she does not get adequate nutrition *in utero*.

- You may wish to enlist the services of a doula, or birth companion. If so, it's best to choose a licensed doula who works for an accredited childbirth service. Doulas can provide emotional and physical support before, during, and after the delivery. In general, doulas will help you find a pathway to empowerment so that you can be involved in the choices affecting your pregnancy and delivery.

- Genetic screenings are available to detect Down syndrome and other possible birth defects. Your healthcare provider can provide you with more information about such screenings.

- Remember to keep your mood and thoughts positive and happy during your pregnancy, from the earliest weeks of the first trimester right up to your delivery. There is strong scientific evidence that your unborn baby can detect whether you are happy or sad, nervous or relaxed, worried or confident. Many doctors and psychologists believe that a pregnant woman's thoughts, likes, and dislikes are imprinted on the developing brain of the baby. Good prenatal care goes beyond nutrition, vitamins, and check-ups and includes monitoring your feelings to give your baby sound emotional develop while he or she is in the womb.

- This is a special time for mother and child to bond in a unique way. As you go through the months of gestation, enjoy all of the planning that mothers and fathers do in anticipation of their new arrival. Immerse yourself in preparing the baby's room, choosing a name, and establishing a plan for how the baby will be cared for when you bring it home from the hospital. Make this a fun and rewarding experience for yourself, your partner, and your baby.

CHAPTER ELEVEN

Birth Plan

We were having a baby girl, and even though we'd been hoping for a boy, we were still over the moon that our baby was healthy and developing normally. My mother said that it was more exciting to dress a girl. The more I thought about it, the more I realized that I could have fun picking out the wardrobe for my little girl from the time of birth to the days she was a toddler and beyond. And many years later, she would want to learn about makeup and—far in the future—ask me about dating, although that task might well fall to her father. I had so much to look forward to that I was overwhelmed with joy every time I thought about what lay ahead. God always gives us exactly what we need, and it was his will that we have a little girl. Thanks to my mom, I could see how well this was going to work out.

In the last week of February, I attended the Aligned and Ready Workshop sponsored by Labor of Love. The workshop covered many topics and was based on the fact that nature has designed a woman's body to give birth. But the stress and modern pace of life, coupled with the way we eat, work, and sit, can throw female anatomy out of alignment, thus rendering the process of birth harder than what nature intended. The primary goal of the workshop is to use various movements to ensure that the baby is perfectly positioned for birth, thus making delivery easier (Aligned and Ready—Optimal Positioning, 2017).

The topics covered in the workshop were: conscious pregnancy and birth; yoga and movement for pregnancy and birth; optimal fetal positioning and the power of the pelvis; ball use for pregnancy during labor and postpartum; breath awareness; labor readiness; and dancing and birth sampling (Aligned and Ready—Optimal Positioning, 2017).

Having a conscious pregnancy and birth means that a woman becomes aware of the changes in her body as opposed to just listening to what the doctor says every few weeks during prenatal visits. This was important for me since my natural inclination as an educator is to know how and why things are happening. Since a woman's body undergoes many changes during pregnancy, women should know why they occur, whether they're caused by hormonal changes or the stretching that occurs in the abdominal area as the baby grows and the womb enlarges with amniotic fluid within the placenta.

Yoga can help prepare a woman for delivery because certain positions help relax the hips while simultaneously strengthening the back, legs, and abdomen. Doing the proper yoga poses can keep all muscles limber and help prevent much of the discomfort that women feel as their gestation progresses. It's common to hear women in their second and third trimesters complain about back and leg pain or say that they're unable to stand for long periods of time. When pregnant, the female body is, in some cases, using muscles that have never been exercised before. It's worth noting that I myself felt great throughout my pregnancy. I may have had trouble *getting* pregnant, but I didn't have a problem staying fit and comfortable during my nine-month pregnancy.

Being aware of one's breathing is very important when pregnant. First, breathing deeply and consciously helps to bring oxygen to the developing baby. As noted, all cells in the human body need oxygen to perform their various functions, and it's paramount for a developing child to get the proper amount of oxygen into its bloodstream so that cell division and organ development can proceed normally. Additionally, practicing breath awareness throughout pregnancy pays huge dividends when it's time for delivery. Releasing breath at the just the right time during a contraction once labor has begun can help gravity move the baby naturally through the birth canal. Learning the correct breathing techniques in birthing classes is therefore essential as part of the entire pregnancy and delivery processes.

Birth balls are another tool used to help position the baby for optimal ease during delivery. The balls come in different sizes so that the expectant mother can sit on top of it with her legs parallel to the floor. The ball should give a little under the weight of the mother's body and therefore be slightly soft (Birth Balls, 2017).

Labor readiness is about helping the body to open up, especially if the woman has never given birth before. It's about finding your "birthing body" and making sure that the muscles and organs, including the uterus and the pelvis, are in shape and correctly aligned to allow for an easy birth experience for mother and child.

Dancing for birth starts off with women standing in a circle and giving positive affirmations about birth and mothering. This is another aspect of the mind-body connection, creating positive thoughts about the entire experience of delivery. It is also concerned, like some of the exercises above, with proper fetal positioning. The class uses belly dancing, as well as African and Latin moves, in order to facilitate the hips in opening so that the baby will smoothly drop down into the proper position for a natural delivery (Dancing for Birth Classes. 2017).

I found all of the above classes very helpful as well as enjoyable. They enabled me to connect with other women who were expecting, provided valuable information about the birth experience, toned my muscles, and helped me become healthier through yoga and dancing. I learned that babies have a hard time moving inside the womb and that the exercises described above are designed to help the baby slip out when the time comes. In other words, the goal is for the woman to have a "butter baby" who will encounter no resistance in moving through the birth canal when it announces via contractions that it's ready to enter the world.

In March, I attended the BOLD Wisdom for Birth Workshop, which is when I mapped out my personal birth plan and goal for delivery. BOLD is a program that emphasizes that most of the birth process lies within a woman's thinking and therefore helps her get in touch with her intuitive side and, in turn, her mind and body (BOLD Wisdom for Birth, 2017). It encourages a woman to ask what she wants and expects from the birth experience in its totality. For example, everyone has preconceived notions about being pregnant and giving birth. We see pregnant women and deliveries on television, and almost everyone knows women who have become pregnant, gone to the hospital, and given birth. The entire pregnancy and birth experience is based on simplistic images of women growing larger in the abdomen, experiencing strange food cravings, complaining of back and leg discomfort, and ardently wishing for the day they can go to the hospital and be finished with the entire process. Our cultural attitude towards giving birth is based on the belief that pregnancy is, at first, a great joy but then becomes an annoyance that is to be endured until the gynecologist finally administers drugs to induce labor or perhaps even performs a caesarean section.

BOLD begins with a completely different mindset, which is that women are in control of the process of both pregnancy and the actual birth. This doesn't mean that medicine or medical procedures are excluded from pregnancy and birth, but rather that women can have far more influence over their births than they realize. In more concrete terms, BOLD encourages women to map out specific plans for their births according to their own desires. My birth goals were to have no induction of labor, to have the baby vaginally, and to receive no epidural.

Other features of the program include coping skills and home exercises to emotionally and physically prepare a woman for labor, group discussions, exercises for fetal positioning, and separating fact from fiction in terms of what is culturally believed about the birth process (BOLD Wisdom for Birth, 2017). It should be noted that the BOLD Method for Childbirth was developed by Karen Brody (Brody, n.d.). Karen Brody is also a Love and Intimacy coach.

By March, I was able to see on ultrasound that my baby girl's features were more defined, such as her arms, legs, ears, nose, fingers, and toes. Each time I viewed the ultrasound, it was like looking at a real live miracle in progress, and that's exactly what Nadia Grace was. Decades ago, women who had trouble conceiving had no recourse but to keep trying, with no medical treatments available to overcome their infertility, no online networking to help women find holistic alternatives, and usually no people to encourage them to persevere. Women were far more prone in the past to accept at an earlier age (usually their late thirties) a mindset of resignation and accept either adoption or being childless. Modern medicine and the information available online about infertility may truly be regarded as modern miracles, but I also firmly believe that Nadia Grace was a miracle from God, that it was his divine will that caused her to be conceived. As I looked at the ultrasounds, I realized that a few months earlier she wasn't there—wasn't present inside my body. Now she was. Yes, children are conceived and born because men and women have intercourse, but having gone through so many difficulties in my efforts to become pregnant, I had a definite sense of God's presence in my life, an awareness that everything was happening by design. As far as I was concerned, Nadia Grace was purposely being called to the banquet of life by God himself. I don't demand that other people accept this, but it's what I believed as a woman of faith.

On April 5, Elroy and I took a babymoon to St. Simon Island, Georgia. A babymoon is a relaxing and romantic vacation that couples take, usually in the mother's second trimester, knowing that this will be the final carefree vacation they get to take until their developing child is born, matures, and one day leaves home to go to college or start work. After a baby is born, most vacations are family getaways, which is not to say that couples aren't able to sneak away for romantic trips once in a while. But the fact that their children are home and may have needs is always in the back of their minds for the next eighteen years, so a babymoon is a chance to celebrate the love that produced the baby and relax before it arrives.

Mother's Day arrived, and Elroy gave me roses and a mother-to-be card. I hadn't given birth yet, but I was at twenty-eight weeks and that meant Nadia Grace would soon be making her appearance. It was a special day made more so by a special husband.

I had my first baby shower on May 27. It was a surprise shower thrown after work spearheaded by my sorority sisters Cheryl and Tanzy and was by invitation. I enjoyed every minute of it, soaking up the noise, advice, excitement, and continued encouragement from my colleagues while I waited for baby Fitts to arrive. I was very grateful, and even some of those who couldn't attend sent gifts.

It was also time for another ultrasound, and Dr. Clemmons told me that it would be the perfect time to invite my entire family to get a good luck at the baby. My mother took off work, and the sonogram was also attended by Danielle and her daughter Brooklyn, and Elroy. All went to the doctor's office to have a look at the baby, who was visible on a 4D ultrasound. A 4D ultrasound uses the latest digital technology to show the unborn baby with extreme clarity and, in most cases, in color. Nadia had turned to the correct position for birth, but she wasn't moving and the doctor said she was asleep. Her eyes were closed and her mouth was open. We nevertheless got a good look at her even though we couldn't see her entire face. It was a joyful moment, and I'm glad that my family was there to share it. Dr. Clemmons did his own sonograms, and he burned a DVD of the images so that Nadia, Elroy, and I would be able to see some of her very first moments in the years to come.

Next, I had a second baby shower, this one at Bouldercrest Church of Christ, for friends and church members. It was another enjoyable time and I again received many useful gifts. It was only fitting that I share such an occasion with my faith community since that is where my life had been rooted for so many years.

On June 7 and 8, Elroy and I attended the BOLD Couples Workshop at Labor of Love Doula & Childbirth Services. The two-day class covered many topics, one being how women should identify and then move past fears associated with giving birth (Wisdom for Couples Workshop, 2017). A common fear shared by most pregnant women is the pain associated with childbirth, but as seen above, beliefs about giving birth are often the result of mistaken cultural attitudes perpetuated through the ages. The workshops at Labor of Love are designed to help women move beyond cultural misinformation and, through various techniques, help them enjoy a delivery that is as comfortable as possible.

Other topics covered were developing a plan that spoke to my birth vision and finding a personal voice to make decisions about the birth process. My birth vision included listening to music during the delivery rather than having drugs administered for pain. I was also encouraged to visualize the exact time of day that I would deliver and who would be in the room when the time came.

Avoiding dystocia was also addressed. Dystocia is a difficult birth resulting from the baby not being in the correct position, a small maternal pelvis, or the failure of the uterus to contract properly. Many of the tools from the other workshops were discussed, these being designed to position the baby correctly and make sure that the uterus and surrounding muscles would be toned and ready for delivery through use of yoga, breathing techniques, and birth balls.

Relaxation tools were covered, including massage, aromatherapy, dimmed lights in the birthing room, and other tools that are a matter of individual preference. Even Christmas lights are sometimes used (Wisdom for Couples Workshop, 2017).

Finally, discussions were held about asking questions of the doctors, especially if there were complications with the birth. For example, what was the likelihood that a caesarean section might be needed, or what medical procedures might be necessary if the birth did not go exactly as planned?

With school out for the summer, I had a third shower at the Hilton Garden Inn Hotel on June 13, hosted Dr. B., Danielle and Kierra. This shower was open to even more people since not everyone could attend the previous showers at my school or church, those being geared more for co-workers and those in my church respectively. This was a grand affair, and people even came from out of town to be with my family, friends, church members, sorority sisters and co-workers. Many people, like my friend Angela, had not been able to attend my wedding but had wanted to be present at my baby shower even before I became pregnant, and that request had stuck with me. We all danced, played games, and had an amazing time. Everyone was very excited for me, although not everyone had known of the longstanding struggles I'd had to get pregnant. Some did, but I hadn't wanted to broadcast my situation to everyone over the past three years.

It was Father's Day and I gave Elroy a father-to-be card. He'd stood by me, and I had no doubt that he always would. He was going to make a terrific dad for Nadia Grace.

In June, I switched to Intown Midwifery for my prenatal care since its policies and practices were more in line with my birth plan. They only delivered at Atlanta Medical Center, however, which meant I had to change from Alliant and Dr. Clemmons to a new physician, Dr. Jeffries.

Intown Midwifery was the ideal choice for me since it offered care for the whole woman and encouraged women to have the birth experience they desired. In this sense, Intown Midwifery was a perfect match with Labor of Love Doula & Childbirth Services. At the end of pregnancy, Intown Midwifery uses certain techniques, such as hydrotherapy, fetal positioning, and overall labor support while employing medical interventions when required. In fact, by collaborating with medical doctors, the service is able to handle gestational diabetes, hypertension, obesity, breech births, and other medical complications. All the midwives worked at Atlanta Medical Center (Obstetrical Pregnancy, 2015).

As my delivery date drew closer, I went to appointments at my new OB/GYN's office and to the midwives once a week. I'd planned my pregnancy and birth experience in detail, and everything was falling into place. Hopefully, Nadia Grace would do the same—literally!

Summary and Points to Remember

I knew I was having a girl, and Elroy and I chose the name Nadia Grace. As the months progressed, I could see Nadia's organ and limbs develop normally and knew I was going to have a healthy baby. In May, my family gathered at Dr. Clemmons's office so that we could witness a 4D Ultrasound.

I also attended two workshops at Labor of Love to formulate a specific birth plan by using the mind-body connection. In order to continue this natural approach to childbirth without foregoing normal prenatal care, I switched to Intown Midwifery, where I would be seen by a medical doctor as well as midwives in the final weeks of my pregnancy.

Using the services of Labor of Love and Intown Midwifery allowed me to retain my proactive approach to everything related to getting pregnant. I had been proactive in seeking methods to conceive for three years, and the above services allowed me to continue being an active participant in my care.

During this time period, I was given three baby showers, all of which were fun and allowed me to share the impending birth with family, friends, church members, and co-workers. I didn't experience any discomfort during pregnancy and, thanks to the services mentioned above, was able to set forth a definite plan that conformed to the birth experience I envisioned. It was a wonderful time in my life, and rather than being worried and tense, I was able to relax, work at my job, and enjoy the experience that I'd dreamed about for so many years.

Here are the points I want you to remember from this chapter.

- There are many birth centers around the country. Although women have traditionally prepared for the births of their children by only going to their OB/GYN appointments, there are now birth centers, many affiliated with major hospitals, which offer classes, doulas, and midwives in order to personalize the birth experience and augment traditional medical treatment.
- Birth centers can help you formulate a birth plan to aid in toning and strengthening the pelvic muscles, positioning the baby for a smooth delivery, exploring methods of pain relief without using drugs, teaching breathing techniques that help with pregnancy and delivery, and using dance and yoga to keep the hips loose and open up so that the baby can be well-positioned to drop into the birth canal when it's time for delivery. Many other services, as described in this chapter, can help you prepare for delivery and take the stress out of giving birth by providing you with information that helps separate fact from fiction.
- Retaining the services of a doula or midwife can give you access to trained birth professionals so that you can ask questions and receive more support during pregnancy. The more resources you enlist, the greater contact you'll maintain with birth professionals, giving you greater peace of mind throughout your pregnancy.
- Allow your husband or partner to participate in your prenatal care and to attend classes or workshops. The more involvement your partner has in the entire birth experience, the easier it will be for you as a couple to

transition into being parents. Even though you may be the one carrying the baby, your partner should have just as much knowledge about the birth experience as you do. He can better care for you and also have his own peace of mind about what is a life-altering event.

- Ultrasound technology has become highly advanced. You can now know more about your baby's development and health from looking at a sonogram than was possible just twenty years ago. Also, new technology such as 4D and HD ultrasounds can give extremely clear pictures of your baby *in utero*, often in color, that are transferred to a DVD so that a baby's development can be preserved indefinitely.

- Allow your relatives to view an ultrasound so that they can share in your joy. Doing so strengthens family ties and allows the baby to enter a close-knit family structure once he or she is born. Just as it's important to include your partner in prenatal care during pregnancy, it's important to allow your family to know about your birth plan and what can be expected once the baby is born.

CHAPTER TWELVE

Baby Fitts

In July, I contacted Teresa to arrange for what is called Placenta Encapsulation Services. The placenta is literally what the baby is encased in during a woman's pregnancy and is the interface for the exchange of blood, oxygen, nutrients, and waste between mother and child. In nature, most mammals consume their placentas after birth for its nutritional value, and for many generations the Chinese have been creating a palatable form of the human placenta by steaming and dehydrating it so that it can be put into the form of powder, pills, or capsules.

Holistic medicine advocates placenta encapsulation for several reasons: it has the potential to decrease postpartum depression; it increases the presence in the bloodstream of oxytocin, a hormone that helps the uterus to heal after delivery and return to normal size; it restores iron levels to normal; it increases milk production in the mother; and it replenishes the body with much-needed B vitamins (Placenta Encapsulation, n.d.).

The time for me to give birth was drawing near, and my birth plan was firmly in place. During my routine prenatal visit on July 7, it was discovered that my amniotic fluid was low, which meant that Nadia was probably going to come a little earlier than expected. Low amniotic fluid is medically known as ologohydramnios. During pregnancy, amniotic fluid levels gradually increase until weeks thirty-four to thirty-six, after which they begin to decline as birth approaches. Other factors, however, can contribute to low amniotic fluid. The most common reason for a decrease in the fluid is that the mother may have become dehydrated, especially during the summer (and recall that this was July). Also, the baby may swallow more of the fluid as gestation draws near to term (Dekker, 2016).

I called Teresa, who advised me to take some common sense measures, such as drinking more water and soaking in a pool to increase my amniotic fluid levels. I tried both, however my amniotic fluid level was still not a satisfactory level. The good news was that Nadia, for all intents and purposes, was at full term, and I'd made it through the entire pregnancy with virtually no pain, morning sickness, or discomfort. But with my delivery date drawing near, I was afraid and excited all at the same time. It wasn't that I'd lost confidence, but rather it was a case of normal human jitters since birth is a major event in the life of the mother and baby. I'd been practicing for the big day in many ways by using the techniques I'd learned in the Labor of Love workshops, and now it was time to use the ones specifically for delivery. I suppose it's no different than an athlete who has practiced for weeks or months for a big sporting event. He may feel confident and relaxed during pre-game workouts, but when game time comes, he or she usually has a few butterflies due to anticipation. Will he perform up to his potential? Will he remember all of the things his coaches have instilled in him?

The first thing I did was to call my mother, close family, friends, and co-workers, these being the individuals who'd known about my pregnancy and struggles to conceive. Elroy's dad, whose birthday is on July 10, came from Littleton so that he could be present when Nadia arrived.

I was admitted to the hospital on July 8. Dr. Jeffries had been checking on my dilation and it was noted that my blood pressure was elevated. I walked from the doctor's office to the hospital—it was just a short distance since the office complex was near the hospital as is the case with many clinics these days—and in the time it took me to make that brief trip, my blood pressure returned to normal. The high reading hadn't been the result of diabetes or preeclampsia, but rather my own stress since everything was starting to happen so quickly. Despite the normalization of my blood pressure, I still needed to be admitted to the hospital because of my low amniotic fluid.

Once admitted, I prayed over the phone for a successful delivery with Brother Woods, who is an elder at my church, and with Diana and her husband Pastor Porter, minister at Mount Zion AME-Kennesaw. God had brought me this far, and just because I'd had a successful pregnancy didn't mean that he was finished his work. Indeed, God's work is never-ending on behalf of his children. He'd been with me every step of the way since I was born—in my childhood, career, dating, marriage, and trying to conceive—and it was time to pray that Nadia might have a blessed and safe entry into the world.

I was admitted so that labor could be induced even though my birth plan had not included induction, but it was deemed medically necessary because of my low amniotic fluid. From within, Nadia herself was sending us a message: "I'm ready!" I didn't inform everyone I knew about what was happening—my circle of friends was quite large—since I didn't know how long induction might take. Induction started on July 8, but I didn't give birth right away. Over the course of the next six days, Teresa, the midwives, and the nurses at the hospital were awesome. Teresa helped me keep my birth plan in focus, the induction notwithstanding, and I kept receiving medication to induce labor.

The magic moment turned out to be 4:29 a.m. on July 13, 2015. Nadia Grace was born vaginally without the need for an epidural. At age forty, I had a healthy baby girl! Nadia was placed on my chest, I was overwhelmed and cried tears of joy. It was an OMG moment if ever there was one. In exhorting his disciples to have greater faith, Jesus told them to always persevere—to keep asking, seeking, and knocking—and I had persevered for many years to make this moment happen. God had heard my prayers and given me a great blessing, a human life, and I was all the more grateful since I had tried so hard to conceive since getting married. But here was my gift from God, a bundle of grace and love who was warm and safely wrapped and lying in my arms. I couldn't have asked for anything better in that moment.

As Jesus said in John 16:21, "A woman giving birth to a child has pain because her time has come; but when her baby is born she forgets the anguish because of her joy that a child is born into the world." It had been a long journey, but the joy I experienced now made up for all the waiting, the various medical treatments I'd undergone, the holistic measures, and the miscarriage.

I was released from the hospital the next day, July 14, and took Nadia home. My sister Danielle watched Nadia in her room down the hall for the first few nights so I could get some rest, although I was too excited the first night and didn't sleep at all. My mom took a week off so she could also help out, and the postpartum assistance I received from family made the homecoming a glorious experience. Elroy had to work the first few days Nadia was home, he was off the following week because he had taken off the week of July 21 (her projected due date).

The housekeeper had cleaned everything at home before I left the hospital, so when we brought Nadia Grace home, the transition to a new life and a baby in the house was seamless. After my sister and mother left, I was on maternity leave so that I could heal and bond with Nadia. I had to adjust to a new schedule, but Nadia was a good baby in that she slept through the night early, ate on time, and didn't cry very much. Night feedings naturally meant that my sleep was disrupted, but it didn't really impact my energy. I guess that I had extra adrenaline since I was so excited to begin this new phase of life, and I kept thinking every single day that I'm *supposed* to be a mother! This was the feeling I'd had for so many years, especially the prior three, and now I was able to begin living the vision that I'd had, the same one I'd made concrete in my visualizations during the Oprah weekend event.

The one sad note at the time was that my friend and co-worker who had brought me breakfast and TLC when I was pregnant, Joycelyn Reid, passed away two months before Nadia was born. The last words she said to me were that she would be at my baby shower in June, but she passed in May 2015. I still miss her, but I know that she is with the Lord and looking down on my family even now.

During the day I could watch television, nap, or simply tend to Nadia's needs and care for her like all new mothers. Elroy worked downstairs, and he was always there if I needed him. It was a great time, and when it was time for me to go back to work, I missed Nadia dearly and cried on the way to school. It was a comfort, however, knowing that she was with Elroy, who could watch her since he worked out of his office at home.

It was wonderful to watch her develop over the months, and social media was a great way to capture all of her "firsts," all of those milestones such as the first time she could hold her head up, focus her eyes, smile, bounce up and down in her walker, and many more. (Later there would be her first steps and first words.) My family and friends were elated to be able to share in Nadia's first moments so easily. All they had to do was go to my wall to see what Nadia was doing on any given day. Recording these special occasions on social media websites, I was creating an indelible record that I could share with Nadia herself as she got older.

My mom and sister were helpful and comforting all during the first year of Nadia's life. If Nadia got sick or if I had any questions about her development, they were always there for me. They also visited on weekends, allowing me and Elroy to have date nights, go to dinner at a nice restaurant, see a movie, or attend football games. Their support helped us strike a good balance between caring for Nadia and maintaining our own relationship. The first year can be hard on many couples who don't have such resources, but we were lucky to have a close and supportive family.

We kept Nadia at home for the first six weeks so as not to expose her to bad weather or germs. This was a time to keep her safe and secure, and I was busy bonding with her during my maternity leave. There was no reason for her to leave home since everything was just as it should have been. My baby was home and I was going to savor every minute of it.

In September, however, we took Nadia to church on Sunday for the first time. Many of the church members had already seen Nadia on Facebook, but happy to see her in person. More importantly, my church was where my entire life of faith was anchored, a faith that had caused me to stay the course for three years and listen to the voice of God as well as the encouragement of the elders and my pastor. It was another milestone and one that many people might not regard as special, but it was for me. It was as if I were bringing my child to the Lord just as Mary and Joseph brought the infant Jesus to the temple to be presented to God shortly after he was born. I was not only perpetuating a family tradition, but it was as if I was bringing Nadia straight to the source that had given her to us to begin with. It seemed only fitting that I should bring her to God's house to say "Thank you."

In October, Nadia won the Annual Neighborhood Halloween Festival. She was dressed as a pumpkin, and I was a proud mother—and it wouldn't be the last time. Nadia looked very cute, and the night was a lot of fun.

The Rogers and Fitts had always been sports-living families, and we brought Nadia to her first Falcons game in November. The Falcons beat the Redskins, and Nadia was well-behaved. She slept through much of the game despite the crowd's cheering, although she was awake part of the time. She didn't cry or seem disturbed by all the commotion around her. Perhaps all of my positive thinking during my pregnancy gave her this kind of indomitable spirit since one would normally expect babies to cry and be frightened by so many people surrounding them. I can only speculate, but I think that I passed along my confidence and sense of peace to her while she was in my womb. Hopefully, she has also inherited a love of sports and the Falcons! She has more than a few red and black outfits with the Falcons' logo. I think it's a safe bet that she'll grow up to be a Falcons fan.

For Thanksgiving, we took Nadia to Enterprise and Opp. It was fitting to take her to the places where I grew up and where, if you recall, my mom and her siblings had lived. This was the first time that most of my family members had seen her, and they were all thrilled to see my little miracle. It goes without saying that I had a lot to be thankful for on Nadia's first Thanksgiving. Since I had such a large family, we gathered for Thanksgiving at a local Church of Christ, where I had visited frequently so many years earlier. In Opp, my aunt Martha (my dad's sister) and cousins was able to see her for the first time.

I should mention that shortly after Thanksgiving, Nadia was with us in front of the TV to watch the Alabama Crimson Tide play the Auburn Tigers with a "Roll Tide" shirt. As I said, she's destined to be a sports fan!

For Christmas, we took Nadia to Littleton so that Elroy's family could see her and become part of the Fitts Christmas morning tradition. We were back where people went to bed early and got up equally as early to exchange gifts and eat breakfast. Though still very young, Nadia was able to use her tiny hand to tear open the wrapping on one of her gifts. We were back where everything had started since this was where Elroy had gotten on his knee and proposed to me on Christmas morning.

All of these various outings and trips represented life events coming full circle. Going to church, a Falcons game, or to visit my family and Elroy's brought Nadia back to places that were not only special but that, in one way or another, represented how Nadia got her start in life. For me, tradition runs deep, which is why I opened this book with my childhood and background. Nadia will undoubtedly become her own person, but there's a saying about history: you don't know where you're going unless you know where you've been. I'm proud to say that Nadia will grow up with a strong sense of who her family members are and what they stand for.

It was cold on New Year's, and Elroy and I didn't feel like going anywhere with Nadia. We'd made the rounds for the holidays, but now it was time for our immediate family to be together: Elroy, Nadia, and myself. The previous year had seen us ring in the New Year with Chandra Currelley and her band as we experienced the first weeks of my pregnancy. This year we would be in our warm and cozy home for a quiet celebration. We were safe and together, and that's the way it should have been. It was also a time to reflect on how far we'd come. In the space of a year, our lives had been given new meaning, and I have no doubt that each new year from here on out will continue to bring us special gifts as Nadia grows and matures. At midnight, as the countdown to 2016 progressed on television, I recorded Nadia, who was awake, to mark her first entrance into a new year. She was almost six months old and developing rapidly.

On Valentine's Day, Nadia wore a red and white outfit to church. On St. Patrick's Day she wore a shirt that said DADDY'S LUCKY CHARM.

In April, we took Nadia on a family trip to Hilton Head, South Carolina, during spring break. My mother took off so she could join us, and we were also accompanied by my niece Brooklyn. Nadia looked adorable in her bathing suit, shades, and flip flops. My mother was able to handle babysitting duties in the evenings so that Elroy and I could go out and have some time for ourselves. It was the best of both worlds and the perfect vacation.

The school year ended in May, and I was free to spend more time with Nadia again, not that Elroy didn't pitch in whenever he was available and needed. In fact, Nadia is indeed "Daddy's Little Girl." She lights up when he enters the room, and the two will even laugh and head butt for fun. It shows how much they love one another. She's a bit of a daredevil and likes to jump from the ottoman. Perhaps she gets this attitude from generations farther back in my family or Elroy's.

I love to dress Nadia, style her hair, and make her into a "girly girl." She has more clothes than I know what to do with, and they were all laid out months earlier so that she would wear outfits at least once. At one point I had to tell my mother to stop buying her new clothes (my mom has enjoyed Nadia as much as any loving grandmother) since she bought a majority of Nadia's wardrobe.

Nadia's first birthday party was at Catch Air. The theme was Mickey and Minnie Mouse—some things never go out of style—and Minnie came out first and pleased everyone! Nadia's grandfather, Eddie Fitts, came from Littleton and baked her a chocolate cake as he does for all of his grandchildren each year. It's a tradition, one among many, that my daughter is lucky enough to be part of.

Nadia started daycare when she was one year old, and it took a few weeks for her to adjust. There was some crying and separation anxiety at first, but this passed quickly and she enjoyed interacting with the other children. Her socialization with students and playmates at daycare has been very positive.

It had been a wonderful first year. Thank God, there had been no major crises or illnesses except the usual sniffles and a few trips to the doctor's for a checkup or her shots. She developed normally in every way and enjoyed being a part of my family and Elroy's. If the first year was any indication of things to come, the years ahead hold a promising future for my daughter.

Summary and Points to Remember

I was admitted to the hospital when it was discovered that my amniotic fluid was low. While this condition is normal in the final weeks of pregnancy, it was a strong indication that our baby was on the way. While there are measures to take to increase amniotic fluid, I was told that it would be necessary to be hospitalized so that induction could begin. While this wasn't part of my birth plan, I was excited that I'd carried my baby full term. Thanks to my preparation, my birth was easy, and Nadia Grace was born on July 13, 2015.

We brought Nadia home from the hospital the day after she was born, with my mother and sister helping out for the first few days so I could rest. During maternity leave, I bonded with Nadia, reveling in being what I'd been destined to be for so long: a mother. Nadia was a good baby, slept through the night, and didn't cry very much. She was the perfect baby in more ways than one.

I posted about Nadia on social media and hope to one day share these posts with her when she's old enough to appreciate them. I also have a photographic record of all her "firsts," such as her first church visit, Halloween, Thanksgiving, Christmas, New Years, Valentine's Day, St. Patrick's Day, and her one-year-old birthday party.

As I write this book, Nadia Grace continues to grow and be a delight to her father and me. I had asked God for a baby, and although I had to wait, when he came through with an answer, he gave me someone who is unique and special!

Here are the points I want you to recall from this chapter.

- Have a postpartum plan in place so that you can make a seamless transition to family life when you bring your baby home from the hospital. Ideally, family members can pitch in during the first week after delivery so that you can get enough sleep and postpartum support. If family members aren't available, childbirth services offer postpartum programs, such as those with doulas, to assist with in-home care for the mother and baby.
- Take advantage of maternity leave when you bring your baby home from the hospital or birthing center. Most employers give women the time they deserve to bond with their newborns after birth, although the time allotted varies from state to state. You should look ahead in order to

know how much time you will receive for maternity leave so that your postpartum plan will be in place when birth and delivery are complete.

- Encapsulation is a method whereby mothers can ingest the nutrients from their placenta in the palatable form of pills and capsules. The nutrients and B vitamins can help a mother recover from birth faster and give her body the boost that only nature itself can provide. You can find out more about encapsulation by talking to your doula, midwife, or childbirth service.

- Be sure to take your child for regular medical checkups and vaccinations. Give him or her the same level of care that you gave yourself during pregnancy.

- Savor the moments of your child's beginnings in life. First moments are just that: they only come once, and it's important to capture these for yourself and your child. It will help to remind your child of how much you loved them after they came into the world and will give them a sense of how special they are.

- Consider using social media to share your child's special moments. It's a great way to enable friends and relatives who live far away to see your baby and to keep your family (and your partner's family) involved in your child's growth and first activities.

- Keep alive the traditions of your family, regardless of what they are. Traditions vary from family to family, but whatever they may be, passing them onto your child represents a giant step towards continuing your traditions well into the future. Traditions build strong families and help instill values in children.

- Be thankful for your child and remember the precious gift that God has given you. If you are one of the many women who has had trouble conceiving and carrying a child to term, give thanks to God on a daily basis and cherish every moment you spend with the new addition to your family. All children are miracles, and if you have successfully overcome infertility, never forget who brought you through your struggles.

CHAPTER THIRTEEN

Mustard Seed Faith

I've taken you through my journey, and as you've seen, realizing the vision you have for your life isn't always easy and takes time. For me, my personal vision consisted of many parts—getting an education, finding a job, buying a home and car, moving to the city, dating, getting married, and having a baby—and it all took many years. Much of the story I've shared with you is about having a baby later in life and struggling with infertility. Coping with infertility and finding strategies to overcome it involved a lot of expensive and complicated medical procedures, and I included them within the context of my life story so that you, the reader, can see what such a struggle is like in the midst of coping with work, travel, family, and all the things that every one of us has to cope with. Nothing in our lives ever happens in a vacuum. I'd always wanted a baby, but my personal vision when I was growing up and then later, when starting to work a full-time job, certainly didn't include terms like intrauterine insemination or in vitro fertilization. It also didn't include fertility monitors and fertility drugs. But I was determined to overcome these obstacles, which took time, research, patience, and faith.

One of the biggest obstacles I encountered was getting over my miscarriage. While it's a common medical occurrence, there can be a stigma attached to it since the norm is for women to marry, get pregnant, and have children. If a woman has a miscarriage, some people may say, "Isn't that a shame! I wonder if she can still have children." It's an understandable reaction, but for the woman and her partner, it can be devastating. A woman might start to think that she's less of a woman, that something is wrong with her since she's not part of the statistical majority. Some women suffer pronounced fear, guilt, and shame for what is a biological reality that affects more individuals worldwide than any of us can possibly know. We don't always hear about miscarriages because women don't want to reveal their personal tragedies while working through the stages of grief. There is no reason to feel shame or humiliation, however. Miscarriages result from medical conditions and biological factors that have nothing to do with self-worth or, in most cases, compromised female reproductive systems. Nobody feels shame because of a broken leg, and women shouldn't feel guilt because they've suffered a miscarriage. It's a part of life that some people have to bear.

It's important to know how to cope with miscarriage and the stigma that often attaches to it. If you've had a miscarriage, you first need to know that it's okay to feel sad and allow yourself to go through the stages of grief. It's normal to be disappointed, but sadness isn't the same thing as shame. Give yourself permission to experience normal human emotion. You should talk about your experience with your partner and remember that he's going through the disappointment as well even though he didn't experience the actual physical process of losing a child. Elroy and I, for example, talked to each other and gave each other support. He was always at my side, saying, "You have time. It's not too late. You're as young as you feel. It's going to happen." If you feel comfortable sharing the experience with your family and your closest friends as well, then do so. Also, don't overlook the comfort and healing that can come from speaking to your pastor, minister, mental healthcare professional, or personal physician. Most of all, remember that having a miscarriage does not automatically mean that you'll never get pregnant again or never have a baby. I encountered many women on my journey who went on to have one or more children after a miscarriage. It's a hard event to weather, but it's not the end of the world.

I also want my readers to know that infertility itself carries a stigma. Infertility afflicts millions of women, but like miscarriage, you don't necessarily hear about a couple's struggle with infertility because there's a certain unwarranted shame or embarrassment that comes with the condition. It's all too common for a woman to feel as if she's abnormal as she watches other women, regardless of their ages, bear children. Why, she may ask, is she the exception? If other couples are successful, why can't she and her partner have a baby together? Whether the issue is miscarriage or infertility, the stigma arises from feeling different, and in our society, being different is too often frowned upon.

And yet the problem of infertility runs deeper than that. One has only to read the Old Testament to see the attitude that having many children (especially strong sons in biblical times) was considered to be a gift from God, a sign of his favor, as well as acceptance by the community. Barren women were often frowned upon or seen as outcasts. Perhaps the problem becomes exaggerated in our own times because there is such an emphasis placed on sexuality and femininity. Being a "real woman" means looking, acting, and feeling like glamorous models on the covers of glossy magazines. It means having the life that the majority of women have. In a society that often judges by appearances, it's easy to become marginalized and suffer low self-esteem if one doesn't look like a swimsuit model. Add in the issue of infertility, and a woman can be overwhelmed if she's "different."

The way to get beyond this stigma is to realize that infertility is a medical condition. No one is judged if he or she has diabetes, high blood pressure, or some other routine medical condition. In the same way, infertility is also a medical condition, but in a majority of cases it can be treated in any number of ways. As seen by my own experiences, infertility can be addressed by diet, exercise, nutrition, vitamin supplements, massage, acupressure, reflexology, and learning more about ovulation and the use of ovulation kits, apps, or monitors. Women who are diagnosed as being clinically infertile can seek help from their OB/GYN or fertility specialists. It may be necessary to consider taking fertility drugs or undergoing IUI or IVF. The most important thing to remember is that there are many options on the table and that infertility is a treatable condition. There have been many medical advancements in the past several decades that mean couples no longer have to automatically choose adoption or say to themselves that having a child just isn't in the cards. Before fertility drugs and the procedures mentioned in this book, these were common "mental default positions," but modern medical technology has given women many different options, and it's premature to throw in the towel and say, "It's too late" if you're in your thirties or forties. It wasn't too late for me, and that's one of the most important reasons why I wrote this book. I want to let women know that they still have a chance to get married and have children even if these events are delayed or don't all happen at once.

The bottom line is that if you're having trouble conceiving or are considered medically infertile, you should do research, consult a medical professional, and learn what's available depending on your own circumstances and personal medical history. Remember that there may be multiple ways to address the problem. I myself explored several avenues, but what finally worked for me may not be the answer for you. I was blessed and finally conceived naturally. Maybe you need to lose weight or take vitamins. Maybe your fallopian tubes are blocked and can be opened again. Then again, perhaps all you need is to have a positive attitude and learn when the best time is to have intercourse. It depends on the individual, but all women who are having trouble conceiving should realize that there are strategies and medical treatments available. No one has to feel as if she is less of a person if she is considered infertile. If counseling is needed, it's available from trained mental healthcare professionals.

I know from personal experience that networking and talking to others helps a great deal. Celestine Beverly, owner of Dendera Cosmetic Studio in Atlanta knew my story and encouraged me along the way since I've gone there for a while, and just like beauty shop and barbershop talk, the women and staff liked to pass along encouraging advice. Since I gave birth to Nadia, it has been amazing how Celestine and others tell women also struggling about my trials and ultimate success, those women who now ask me for advice—even complete strangers who I talk to on the phone, women who find themselves exactly where I was a few years ago: without a husband or a baby. It's gratifying that I can help people since that's what life is all about. I like to think that God helped me, not just for myself, but so that I can help others and be what Jesus called us to be: a city shining on a hilltop.

Many of my friends and family observed my personal odyssey through my Facebook page. Followers tell me that I have offered encouragement and given them hope, and often they tell me that because they persisted or tried one of the many things I have mentioned in the course of these chapters, they, too, have found the right mate or become pregnant. Their enthusiasm and joy have been very gratifying to read or hear about. One Saturday morning in November 2015, shortly after having Nadia God put in on my heart to post words of encouragement in a Facebook Group for Educators. Let me share a post I made in the group, which prompted the kind of responses I receive (and continued to get responses for weeks) because I shared my story. The post was accompanied by a picture of Nadia Grace.

Facebook post:

"Happy Saturday BER! This school year makes my 17th year in education. I started the 2015-2016 school year on maternity leave after having my first baby at the age of 40. Introducing: Nadia Grace, which means (hope & gift from God). One of the reasons I work hard every day of the week. When I come home, she is waiting for me. Coming home to this little face after a day fulfilled with supporting high school teachers & students as a SST/RTI specialist makes me happy. I leave "Dr. Fitts" at the door and become wifey & mommy! #healthybabyat40 #youstillhave time #summerbabiesrock #thankful"

I also told people that I wanted to write a book. The kinds of replies I received (paraphrased) are listed below.

> "That's awesome!"
> "Write that book, girl!"
> ((HUGS))
> "Only God can work miracles like this!"
> "Your post really spoke to me. Thanks!"
> "I thought things were over for me . . . until now."
> "Thank you for sharing. I have new hope!"
> "At 37, I have no boyfriend or family. But I'm not giving up!"
> "You don't know who I am, but I read your post with tears of joy."

These are just a few of the comments I've received, and taken together with those I receive in person, I can honestly say that my story, through the grace of God, has helped many people to have hope, overcome the above stigmas, and dare to believe that miracles (such as husbands and babies) lie in their future. The above post, by the way, received over 200 comments and 4,000 Likes on Facebook. My simple message of joy and thanksgiving resonated with people around the country. That's why I wrote this book with the hope and passion that I put into all other endeavors in my life, including conquering infertility.

Just as I posted on Black Educators Rock and spread my story by word of mouth, I wanted to tell you, my readers, that it's never too late, that there's hope, and that you should use my life experiences and the advice in this book as tools to climb your own mountains and find the lives you want and have dreamt about since you were a child.

While this book is mainly addressed to females, especially those in their later childbearing years, I want to devote some time to my husband and best friend, Elroy Fitts. Without him, my dreams wouldn't have come true. He was standing in my path at the right time, a gift from God who has stood by me and encouraged me with his calm, strong, and assertive voice, always standing behind my can-do attitude and belief that I could achieve my goals. He's the person I was meant to go through life with, and he's the man who was destined to be the father of Nadia Grace. He shared the good times and bad and never lost faith that things were going to work out. He never placed stock in the concept of a biological clock and always believed that we would one day have a baby. He's a great husband and father, a man I can always count on.

If your husband or partner is frustrated because you haven't yet conceived, sit down and have a heart-to-heart talk with him. Ask him to go online and do some research. Have him meet with your doctors or those who have been successful in having a child later in life. Discuss your goals with him, list the options the two of you should consider, and set a date when you would like things to happen. Remember that the two of you are a team, and your journey should represent a joint effort. You don't have to do this alone, and your partner, if reluctant, needs to understand this all-important concept.

Just as Elroy encouraged the side of my personality that is goal-driven, that's what I want to do for you: encourage you to be a goal-driven person who doesn't give up on your dream—ever! You have to engage in basic goal-setting, do status checks periodically to see how much progress you've made, ask yourself what kind of changes your strategy might require, and then persevere.

You also have another partner by your side, and that's God. Throughout my narrative I have alluded to prayer and faith that can move mountains, sometimes called mustard seed faith. That's the final thing I want you to take away from this book: a belief that God can work wonders in your life if only you will make him your partner. You may not think you have faith within you, but a mustard seed is one of the smallest seeds that can be sown in the earth, and Jesus probably chose his phrasing very carefully. He expected his disciples to do great things through faith, including the kinds of things he himself did, from healing the sick to walking across the Sea of Galilee.

Faith, of course, must grow and become strong, but it starts with a single step, a single goal, and a single prayer, no matter how small. You can move mountains if you're determined, set goals, and work on achieving them. But things happen in God's time, not ours, and as my story illustrates, sometimes the answers we're looking for take time to manifest themselves. For me, it took years to find the right man to be my husband. Once I found him, it took three years for us to have a baby. I never gave up, however, and trusted that God was working behind the scenes to answer my prayers. God doesn't wave a magic wand since he's not a magician doing parlor tricks. He knows what to do, but more importantly he knows how and when to answer your prayers. Give him a chance and he'll come through.

If you have trouble accepting this, then I want you to think back on my story, because that's another reason why I've shared my journey with you: to let you know that miracles can happen. I already know it's possible because I came through my trials thanks to a series of coincidences that can't be explained by ordinary means, at least not in my estimation. There are many skeptics who think that everything that happens has a scientific explanation and is the result of cause and effect, but remember that God can use any means he wants to bring something to pass. My challenge to you is to give it a try. Take a deep breath and, like Peter, dare to step out of the boat when Jesus tells you to come across the water.

Is this the end of my journey just because I have my job, a husband, and a baby? Not at all! This book may be complete, but I know there are new goals to achieve in the future. Nadia has many years ahead of her, and I look forward to being her mother for as long as I live. One day, she may have a family of her own, and then I'll become a grandmother, and that will be another dream, another goal, and another gift from God. And if you recall, I've always been interested in the entertainment industry— radio, television, film, and theatre. I will continue to be an educator—another journey that is far from over—but when it is (or perhaps even sooner), maybe I'll have a second career in the entertainment industry. I don't know how it might happen, but I don't put any limitations on myself or God.

I'm sure there are other goals I haven't dreamed of yet. That's okay. New goals will come along as the years go by. I'm confident that I'll be shown how to accomplish them when they do, whatever they might be. Why? Because I have mustard seed faith.

And you can have it, too. You still have time.

THE END

REFLECTIONS

Use the following pages to write down lessons learned and how you plan to apply what you have learned to YOUR PERONAL JOURNEY.

_____

_____

_____

_____

_____

_____

_____

_____

_____

_____

_____

_____

_____

_____

_____

REFERENCES

Aligned and Ready—Optimal Positioning. (2017). Retrieved from https://alaboroflove.org/aligned-and-ready-workshop/

Birth Balls. (2017). Retrieved from http://alaboroflove.org/product/birth-balls/

BOLD Wisdom for Birth. (2017). Retrieved from https://alaboroflove.org/bold-wisdom-for-birth-2/

Brody, K. Bold Method: Our Founder. (n.d.). Retrieved from http://your boldbirth.com/projects/

Dancing for Birth Classes. (2017). Retrieved from http://alaboroflove.org/dancing-for-birth-classes/

Danielsson, K. (2017). Odds of Miscarrying after Seeing Heartbeat on Ultrasound. Retrieved from https://www.verywell.com/miscarriage-heartbeat-ultrasound-odds-2371536

Dekker, R. (2016). What Is the Evidence of Induction for Low Amniotic Fluid in Healthy Pregnancy? Retrieved from https://www.scienceandsensibility.org/p/bl/et/blogid=2&blogaid=503

The Effect of Weight on Fertility. (2016, June 29). Retrieved from www.shadygrovefertility.com/blog/fertility-health/effect-eight-fertility/

Fertility Monitors Can Reduce the Time It Takes to Conceive. (2017). Retrieved from OvaCue.com

Goodlatte, J. (2014, January). A Mother's Emotions Affect Her Unborn Child. Retrieved from http://getfitforbirth.com/a-mothers-emotions-affect-her-unborn-child/

Harmony Prenatal Test. (2017). Retrieved from http://www.ariosadx.com/expecting-parents/

Having a Doula: Is a Doula For Me? (2017). Retrieved from http://americanpregnancy.org/labor-and-birth/having-a-doula/

Hawthorn, K. (2015). The Unquantifiable Benefits of Reflexology for Fertility. Retrieved from http://natural-fertility-info.com/reflexology.html

How Much Does IVF Cost at Chicago, IL? (2017). Retrieved from http://www.advancedfertility.com/ivf-cost.htm

Hysterosalpingogram (HSG). (2012, November 2). Retrieved from http://answers.webmd.com/answers/2000395/what-is-a-hysterosalpingogram-hsg

Infertility and In Vitro Fertilization. (2015, May 22). Retrieved from http://www.webmd.com/infertility-and-reproduction/in-vitro-fertilization-for-infertility

Intrauterine Insemination: IUI. (2017, July 28). Retrieved from http://americanpregnancy.org/infertility/intrauterine-insemination/

IVF Grants. (2014). Retrieved from http://babyquestfoundation.org/

Karras, T. (n.d.). Does Acupuncture for Infertility Work? Retrieved from http://www.parents.com/getting-pregnant/infertility/treatments/acupuncture-for-infertility/

New Family Soothing Sessions. (2017). Retrieved from http://alaboroflove.org/new-family-soothing-sessions/

Obstetrical Pregnancy. (2015). Retrieved from http://www.intownmidwifery.com/why-midwifery/obsterical-pregnancy

Our Classes. (2017). Retrieved from http://alaboroflove.org/classes/

PinkPad User. (2012, January 11). Here Is How to Get Pregnant. Retrieved from https://pinkpad.alt12/community/groups/88/posts/1062119-here-is-how-to-get-pregnant

Placenta Encapsulation. (n.d.). Retrieved from http://americanpregnancy.org/first-year-of-life/placental-encapsulation/

Pollack, A. (2010, January 28). Firm Brings Gene Test to Masses. Retrieved from www.newyorktimes.com/2010/01/29/business/29gene.html

Rodriguez, H. (2017). Prepare for Conception with a Fertility Cleanse. Retrieved from natural-fertility-info.com/prepare-for-conception

Sherbahn, R. (2017). Embryo Quality and Grading. Retrieved from http://www.advancedfertility.com/embryoquality.htm)

Sonohysterography. (n.d.). Retrieved from https://www.acog.org/-/media/For-Patients/faq175.pdf?dmc=1&ts=20170804T2140508138

Weight BMI and Fertility and IVF Success. (2017). Retrieved from www.advancedfertility.com/weight.htm

Will Geritol Multivitamin Increase My Fertility? (2014). Retrieved from http://geritol.com/increase-my-fertility

Wisdom for Couples Workshop. (2017). Retrieved from http://alaboroflove.org/wisdom-couples-workshop

References for or Further Reading

Bobic, K. (2016, May 18). 12 Ways Surviving a Miscarriage Makes You Stronger. Retrieved from https://romper.com/p/12-ways-surviving-a-miscarriage-makes-you-stronger-7317

Brian, K. (2013, July 12). The amazing story of IVF: 35 years and five million babies later. Retrieved from https://www.theguardian.com/society/2013/jul/12/story-ivf-five-million-babies

Five Steps to Renewing Your Mind. (2016, May 26). Retrieved from http://unlockingthebible.org/five-steps-renewing-mind/

Glezer, Dr. (n.d.). Four Steps to Overcome the Stigma of Infertility. Retrieved from http://mindbodypregnancy.com/how-to-overcome-the-stigma-of-infertility/

Kincaid, Ellen. (2015, June 30). Why having kids later is really a big deal. Retrieved from http://www.businessinsider.com/why-delaying-parenthood-and-having-kids-later-is-a-big-deal-2015-6

Newton, T. (2015, August 24). When Your Husband Doesn't Understand Infertility Emotions. Retrieved from http://www.amateurnester.com/2015/08/husband-doesnt-understand-infertility.html

Polycystic ovary syndrome (PCOS). (n.d.). Retrieved from http://www.mayoclinic.org/diseases-conditions/pcos/basics/definition/con-20028841

Whalen, M. (2016, September 13). Removing the Stigma From Miscarriage Retrieved from http://www.insidesources.com/removing-the-stigma-from-miscarriage/

What is a doula? (2017). Retrieved from https://www.dona.org/what-is-a-doula/

About the Author

Dr. Samantha Fitts suffered infertility and miscarriage. She has been married to Elroy for six years. They are the proud parents of Nadia Fitts and live just outside Atlanta, Georgia. Over the past few years, Samantha has motivated other women through the message of this book.

Samantha graduated with top honors from Alabama State University with a Bachelor of Science Degree in Special Education. She earned her Master's Degree in Special Education from Georgia State University in Atlanta. She went on to earn her Education Specialist in Education Leadership from Lincoln Memorial University in Tennessee, and her Doctorate of Education from the Atlanta campus of Argosy University.

Samantha is an Autism/Special Education Specialist in the central office of Atlanta Public Schools. She is also a Reading Endorsement Instructor in Atlanta Public Schools through the Metropolitan Regional Education Service Agency (MRESA). She has been in education for over twenty years.

For more information, visit www.samanthafitts.com

CPSIA information can be obtained
at www.ICGtesting.com
Printed in the USA
FFHW01n1255131018
48758827-52850FF